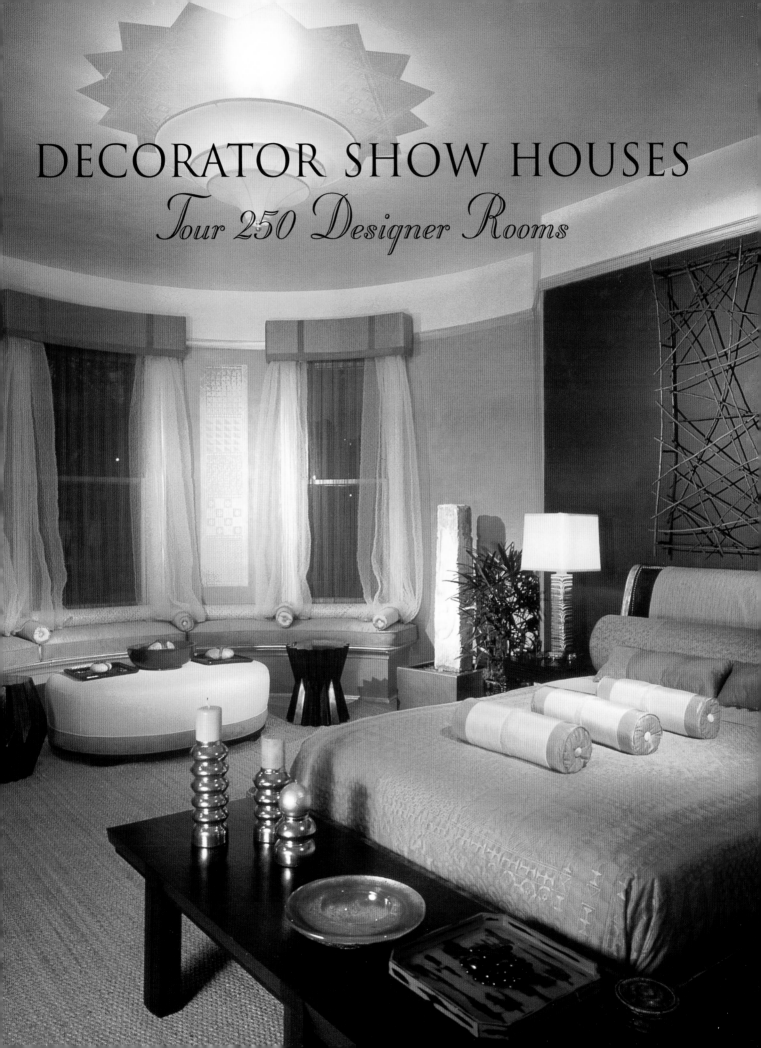

DECORATOR SHOW HOUSES
Tour 250 Designer Rooms

DECORATOR SHOW HOUSES
Tour 250 Designer Rooms

Tina Skinner
Melissa Cardona
Nancy Ottino

Schiffer
Publishing Ltd

4880 Lower Valley Road, Atglen, PA 19310 USA

Library of Congress Control Number: 2004105532
Copyright © 2004 by Schiffer Publishing, Ltd.

Front cover images by John Lewis, David Duncan Livingston, David Schilling, Celia Pearson, and Alise O'Brien. Back cover images by Alexander Vertikoff, Kevin Rose, Lydia Cutter, Bryan Leazenby, and Jeffrey Totaro.
Designed by John P. Cheek
Type set in Trajan/Aldine 721 Lt BT

ISBN: 0-7643-2051-3
Printed in China

Published by Schiffer Publishing Ltd.
4880 Lower Valley Road
Atglen, PA 19310
Phone: (610) 593-1777; Fax: (610) 593-2002
E-mail: Info@schifferbooks.com

For the largest selection of fine reference books on this
and related subjects, please visit our web site at
www.schifferbooks.com
We are always looking for people to write books on new
and related subjects. If you have an idea for a book please
contact us at the above address.

This book may be purchased from the publisher.
Include $3.95 for shipping.
Please try your bookstore first.
You may write for a free catalog.

In Europe, Schiffer books are distributed by
Bushwood Books
6 Marksbury Ave.
Kew Gardens
Surrey TW9 4JF England
Phone: 44 (0) 20 8392-8585; Fax: 44 (0) 20 8392-9876
E-mail: info@bushwoodbooks.co.uk
Free postage in the U.K., Europe; air mail at cost.

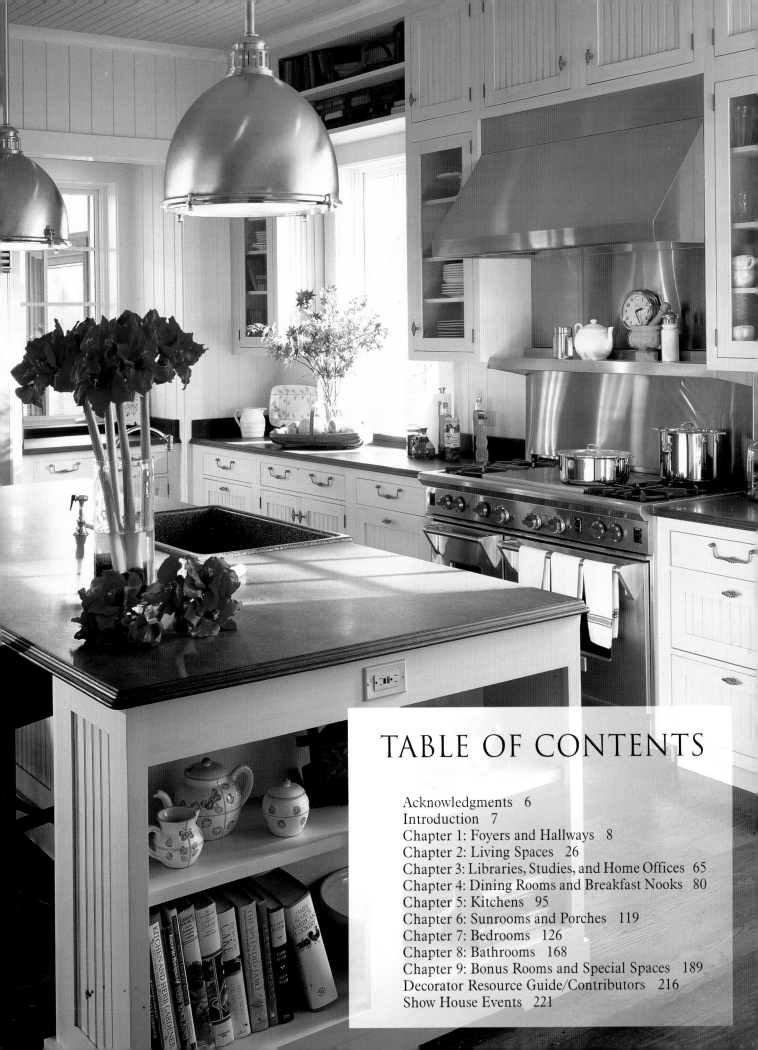

TABLE OF CONTENTS

ACKNOWLEDGMENTS

First and foremost, credit goes to Nancy Ottino, the genius behind the idea for this book.

With regard to the bulk of this book, an enormous chunk of it was made possible by the zealous organization and dedication of the Vassar Show House committee to organize and plan such grand-scale events. Operated annually by the Philadelphia Vassar Club since 1967, the Vassar Show House is the oldest East Coast decorator show house event. Each year, proceeds from the benefit provide financial assistance for area students attending Vassar College, with more than $3 million raised and distributed to well over 800 students. In charge of publicity for the show house for seven years, Susan Wright has been incredibly responsive in helping with the production of this book.

The book is also the cumulative product of over 175 designers' visions, hard work, and resourcefulness.

John Lewis, the committee's "house photographer," has provided an affordable service to the Vassar organizers, applying his talents quickly and efficiently, capturing a slice of every design contribution for posterity. A great big round of applause to him.

Finally, on that note, this book would not be what it is without the talent of all the photographers, who illuminate the art of the designers and make it possible for us to enjoy their work.

INTRODUCTION

Decorator show houses are more than fundraisers and showy exhibitions of interior decorators' work. Over the last half-century, the decorator show house has developed into a rich tradition, spreading across the country and manifesting itself distinctively for each organizing group. The show house is a labor of love, the result of thousands of hours of collective work on the part of organizers, sponsors, and participants, and is often times an integral event in the life of a community.

Decorator show houses are special because the designers get to express themselves, or their imaginary clients, instead of catering (as they do and should) to the needs and tastes of real people. Professional decorators are creative people, even artists, who rarely get a chance to let their inner selves shine. In a decorator show house, not only do they get to let it shine, they get to stand back and watch as hundreds of people parade through their rooms to admire them. It's rare that a decorator is privy to even one private party in most of the homes they so painstakingly detail.

Budgets offer a great deal of leeway, too. In the name of the charitable cause, they can beg and borrow. They can promise their most talented associates (muralists, upholsterers, drape makers) full credit in exchange for help. And they can sell off any items (furniture, accessories) that they need to purchase during the course of the house tour.

So, given the license to fly, the decorators pull out all the stops. The results can be whimsical, elegant, starkly modern, even erotic.

And the feedback! Decorators we interviewed for this book talked about people who returned to the same show house time and again to study the details, hoping to take home something that inspired them and incorporate it into their lives. Most show houses offer "meet the designer" events in addition to regular touring hours, and many of the designers choose to hang out in their rooms, meeting the admirers as they come through, or simply studying their reactions.

While the hard work of participating designers, architects, muralists, and others benefits the charitable cause supported by the show house, it also pays off in terms of generating new business for participants. Many designers in this book claimed to have received more business from show houses than from any other sources. Not surprising, considering the amount of energy, creativity, and resources they heave into the design of a room.

You'll find absolutely amazing rooms in this book. Whether you're a decorator, or just shopping around for design ideas to use in your own home, you will not be disappointed. In fact, you'll be nothing short of inspired. Room by room, this book will take you through impressive foyers, cozy family rooms, grand living rooms, and regal dining rooms. You'll also see magnificent bedrooms, extraordinary bathrooms, and imaginative bonus rooms.

As in any show house, many styles are represented in this book. From ornate and lavishly decorated rooms to ones with sleek contemporary styling, English country to Zen modern, and old world to retro—we've tried to include the best in interior design today. We invite you to visit the resource lists in the back of the book, which contain guides to all the marvelous designers and show houses represented on these pages.

For the price of an afternoon at *one* show house, this book takes you through fifty of them, showcasing hundreds of rooms and innovative design ideas. We're sure that you'll be amazed at what you find.

CHAPTER 1
FOYERS AND HALLWAYS

A Cheerful Welcome
Pickens Homes, LLC
Evansville Living Idea Home 2003

Ten-foot high ceilings and molded archways set the stage for a foyer drenched in wonderful coral paint, warm and welcoming to guests. Black and white marble flooring introduces a classic theme, while the framed botanical prints hint at a gardening motif throughout the rest of the house. An arching, custom-designed spider web window leaves a lasting impression on those who step up to the full mahogany front door.

Lush Landing
Castellina Interior Design Studio
Vassar Show House 2002

Gilded furnishings, crystal lighting, and an abundance of muted texture in the carpet, wall, and window treatments add up to grand for this impressive entryway.

Photography by David Kreutz and Associates

Photography by David Kreutz and Associates

Photography by David Kreutz and Associates

With only a few windows in this entry hall and balcony, the designers felt a special challenge to make the space brighter. They used an amber gold-brushed faux finish on the walls, achieving the effect of bringing in more sunlight. To create contrast, a dramatic strie faux finish in pomegranate and artichoke was added to the landing and balcony. In order to complement the leaded glass window and immense scale of the space, a "floating" light fixture was custom-designed. Wrapped in translucent fabrics, the fixture was made to resemble hot air balloons to create a whimsical focal point that did not detract from the beautiful Palladian window.

Sophisticated elegance is the name of the tune in this space, designed to be both a music room and entry for a young couple fond of entertaining. Sienna, umber, and hot coral dominate the color palette, exuding a jazzy sensibility and warmth that welcomes guests to sit and listen to the music emanating from the antique Boesendoerfer, or mingle in the open space of the entry.

davidduncanlivingston.com

Entrance Provence
Sorella's Decorating, LLC
Shoreline Foundation Decorators'
Show House 2002

©Olson Photographic, LLC

Walking into the grand central hall is like stepping back in time, to an antique villa in the South of France. J. Andrew Hull Decorative Finishes and Decorative Artist Ashley Cotton teamed up to create walls faux finished to imitate the color of sage moss growing on an old stone wall, and a mural of the French countryside. Tea-stained rugs balance the texture of cool marble floors.

Underwater Foyer
Willem Racké Studio, Inc.
San Francisco Decorator Showcase 2003

Margot Hartford Photography—www.margothartford.com

The home's proximity to the ocean inspired this designer to create an underwater-themed decorative wall mural. Of particular interest is the marvelous floor that was stained and stenciled in a nautical theme with a shell, seaweed, and compass design. The seashell table was custom-designed for the foyer.

Margot Hartford Photography—www.margothartford.com

Arrivals and Departures
Maurice E. Weintraub Architect, Devine Designs, Inc.
Vassar Show House 2002

©John Lewis Photography

Maurice E. Weintraub

Maurice E. Weintraub

A mudroom was engineered around the playful theme of coming and going within the house. The history of the area railroad became the theme, with area rail-line maps and even an aerial photo of the area papered to the ceiling. Related antiques and paraphernalia pack the room, making it a wonderful history lesson.

The Foyer Waiting Room
Bordet Interiors and Susan Harter
Tara Drive Decorator Show House 2003

This room gives visitors a taste of the quality and style of the rest of the house. By mixing different styles of furniture, a comfortable and elegant area was created, keeping within a traditional design and color palette. The walls of the space feature a delicate stenciled design in silver over a base of pale gray. Collections of artwork, fine furniture, and accessories give the impression of a well-traveled occupant. The classical landscape painting by Susan Harter adds softness and romance to the space.

Richard Smith—HaywardSmith Photography

Richard Smith—HaywardSmith Photography

Richard Smith—HaywardSmith Photography

Lofty Retreat
Ethan Allen Evansville
Evansville Living Idea Home 2003

Warm Invitation
NMP, Inc.
Vassar Show House 2003

A window bursting with sunlight makes this upstairs foyer maintain a light and airy nature. Crisp and clean styling defines the comfortable furnishings, which feature a castered Cameo and complimentary Calais upholstered piece with embossed rosettes. The inspiration for the room's design was based on the "coastal cottage" look, with some influence coming from late 18th and early 19th century European influences. The overall look is that of a "high" country style, exuding classic and contemporary elegance.

A spacious entry foyer doubles as office space, where the mail lands, and bills are paid before being sent back to the post box. Striped/glazed walls contrast with crisp, white wainscoting and trim. A gilded fireplace and faux marble surround also distinguish the room.

Photography by Alexander Vertikoff

Photography by Alexander Vertikoff

Formerly a little-used basement area, the stairway provides a dramatic and exciting entrance that gives light, life, and new purpose to this part of the house. Fiber optic technology and traditional Venetian plaster create a dialogue between new and old.

Photography by Alexander Vertikoff

Showing off his wallpapering skills, Don Larkin's touch is evidenced in floor cloths,
framed art, and even the cabinet – every inch of which sports a subtle paper print.

Why Go Any Further?
Sonja Willman Designs
St. Louis Symphony Show House
and Gardens 2003

An expansive staircase landing with leaded windows lends itself as a quiet place to sip wine, enjoy tea, or get lost in a good book. Soft earth tones combined with rustic textures entice you to put your feet up and get comfortable, and make you forget where you were going.

Back Stair
Devine Designs, Inc. and Maurice E. Weintraub
Architect
Vassar Show House 2001

Can't you almost picture him, sneaking out the back door early in the a.m. for a golf getaway? A lot of research and energy was invested in the design. Golf cartoonist and artist, Charles Crombie's work was adapted for the wallpaper border, recalling the former Tredyffrin Country Club and Golf Links that once covered 135 acres near the show house.

World-Tour Gallery
Designers Furniture Outlet
Vassar Show House 2001

A spacious upper foyer crowns a grand staircase. The designers chose a rich, multi-layered mix of neutral colors, luxurious textures, and eye-catching details. Treasures from abroad, and European-inspired fabrics, tapestries, and furnishings evoke past travels.

A Living Hall
Bruce Norman Long Interior Design
Princeton Junior League Show House 2002

This grand entrance hall in a colonial revival home was very much the "family room" of its day. It is decorated in a summery mode of slipcovered furniture arranged for playing games, reading, or taking a nap. Crisp white wainscoting and grass green walls are fresh backdrops to a stately antique grandfather clock, gilded girandole mirror, and a Chippendale style sofa. A multicolored wool stripe carpet unifies the meandering space from front door to garden door and coat rack to fireplace nook.

Photography by Stewart O'Shields

Photography by Stewart O'Shields

Biblioteque
Jeffrey Dean, Ltd.
Vassar Show House 2001

A small corner in an upstairs hall offers the first place for picking out the next book. Palm-covered fabrics screen the books from dust, and a towering clock shares the hour with the entire household.

Victorian Entry
Linda Wiley Interiors
Vassar Show House 1999

A wax figure of a butler offers a generous greeting in this entry hall, where bronze greyhounds guard antique furnishings. A custom ottoman land accent pillows add contemporary flair to the setting. Looking up, a hand-painted border circles a coffered ceiling.

Elegant Impressions
Taylor Wells Design
National Symphony Orchestra
Decorators' Show House 2002

This entry hall echoes the style and grandeur of an earlier time. Because every room in the home flows in and out of the space, neutral cream tones were used for the color palette. Original pilasters marbleized in black, with Corinthian capitals in antique gold leaf add to the sense of history, as does the classically inspired bronze statue of Mercury. The stairs were carpeted with Belgian wool and the windows were dressed in Oriental silk plaid fabric to add richness and elegance.

CHAPTER 2
LIVING SPACES

Naturally Great Room
Richar Interiors Inc.
Chicago Home and Garden Design House 2003

The designer took his cue from nature and filled the room with
multiple textures and patterns to achieve a casual European flavor.

Photography by David Schilling

Era Indefinite
Susan Dearborn Interiors, Inc.
The JCC Designer Show House 2002

Set in an 1850s Federalist home, the room is yesterday in warmth, today in style. Texture, scale, and a harmonious color palette blend through a mixture of old and new pieces.

A Romantic Age
Lea Matthews Furniture & Interiors
Evansville Living Idea Home 2003

Bryan Leazenby/OnSite Images for Evansville Living Magazine

Bryan Leazenby/OnSite Images for Evansville Living Magazine

Casual elegance defines the choice of fabrics used in this family room. The light green Century sofa is reminiscent of the Romantic Age with its beautifully carved arms and feet, and provides the centerpiece around which the rest of the furnishings revolve. Two Hickory Chair end tables with a Grecian flair strike a balance with the entertainment wall unit on the other side of the room. Greenery and a botanical print also serve to balance the color scheme of the room.

Bryan Leazenby/OnSite Images for Evansville Living Magazine

Botanical Living
People's Furniture
Evansville Living Idea Home 2003

Warm, coral accents provide a striking contrast to the cooler greens and yellows throughout this living room. The spider-back chair is upholstered in green, drawing out the green in the rug, which covers a lovely hardwood floor. Botanical prints with black frames are anchored by the fireplace's black marble. Overall, the room displays a traditional sensibility, while maintaining a contemporary appeal.

Bryan Leazenby/OnSite Images for Evansville Living Magazine

Bryan Leazenby/OnSite Images for Evansville Living Magazine

Studious with a Smile
Inside Outlook Custom Interiors
Vassar Show House 2003

©John Lewis Photography

The sofa sports sheep, the shelves a great personal collection of porcelain. The point is that an area designed for comfortable family living should evoke smiles, so the designers infused this space with bright light and friendly colors.

An Intimate Soiree
Bloomingdale's Design Studio
Vassar Show House 2003

Envisioned as the perfect place for an aperitif, this room was draped in a luxurious combination of fabrics and trims. Billowing silk frames the windows like a lady's ball gown.

©John Lewis Photography

Traditional with a Modern Twist
Alexander Blank Fabrics, Inc.
Baltimore Symphony Associates Decorators'
Show House 2003

Photography by John Coyle Jr., Baltimore MD

A chunky stylish tattersal check, a vividly enlarged tartan plaid, and a bold, grand hound's-tooth weave adorn this unique and enticing living space. The spectacular exchange of textures and colors including crisp apple greens, pineapple yellows, watermelon pinks, and tangerine oranges creates a fruitful ambiance. Classic furniture with a fresh, clear approach to color and patterns coupled with bold graphic elements embrace creativity and style…Exhilarating…Energetic.

Photography by John Coyle Jr., Baltimore MD

Venetian Morning
Penelope Rozis
San Francisco Decorator Showcase 2001

The designer used contrasting materials to make this room more interesting. The elegant hand-printed cotton Fortuny fabric, antique Oushak rug, and the antique gold leaf mirrors were used along with white burlap curtains with Fortuny trim along the leading edge. The "pali" table legs and curtain rods were used to add a touch of humor to the space.

Freshly Feminine
Melanie Ward, Inc.
Shoreline Foundation
Decorators' Show House 1999

©Olson Photographic, LLC

©Olson Photographic, LLC

This designer wanted to create a space rich in elegance and comfort. A mix of brightly colored fabrics, casual furnishings, and refined accessories creates a room that is inviting. Floral prints and cheery colors add a freshly feminine feel to the room.

Green Bada-bing
Design Express, Ltd.
Vassar Show House 1999

John Martinelli Photography

A space was brightened and cheered with a two-tone, blue and apple green scheme of textiles. Creating an entire length of rippling fabric was a less expensive alternative to removing the orange-colored paneling and refinishing the wall. Repeating patterns and colors make the room seem more open, and an unexpected check pattern adds snap to the repeating flip-flop treatment of toile.

John Martinelli Photography

John Martinelli Photography

John Martinelli Photography

John Martinelli Photography

John Martinelli Photography

This walk through area off the living room needed an excuse to make people stop and pause. The designers expanded the reading room theme and added an antique harp and a leather game table with chairs, in the process creating the perfect spot for after-dinner conversation with friends. Palm fabric chair covers add exotic flair.

Classically Modern
Jan Kyle Design
Kansas City Symphony Designer Show House 2002

Photography by Wayne Hunthausen

Photography by Wayne Hunthausen

This master sitting room, with three openings to other rooms, a dormer area, and a pink marble fireplace surround, presented a special challenge to the designer. To add sophistication to the room, the fireplace surround was transformed to black marble using a faux painting technique, and the ceiling was painted aqua to give the room a cool feel. A transitional Bedermeier cabinet was installed in the corner to resonate with the 1930s maple chest with ivory and nickel pulls, adding a timeless dimension to the room's design.

An Affair in Paris
Valentine Interiors Design & Decorating Shop
Middlesex County YMCA, Lyman Homestead
Showhouse 2001

son Photographic, LLC

©Olson Photographic, LLC

A spacious room was set with tables for two overlooking the River Seine, where wine and cheese might be served, while someone takes a seat at the grand piano to entertain. Vapor blue walls add outdoor glow to a room where whimsical topiary and animated geese and bunnies cavort among lavishly upholstered furniture and grand scale window treatments.

Inside Out
Knowlton Associates, LLC
Vassar Show House 2000

Sky blue silk on the windows draws in the
surrounding views. Inside, the heavily wooded
grounds beyond are shadowed on the wall in
elegant panel paintings.

Blue Parlor
Group 3
Vassar Show House 2003

Shades of blue, soft yellow, and camel mix to evoke an airy summer room. The use of a sea grass area rug, distressed, hand-rubbed furniture, and bold plaid and striped fabrics reinforces the theme. The focal point of the room is a tall, triple arch bookcase that is hand decorated with soft antique designs and colors.

San Francisco Mélange
Penelope Rozis
San Francisco Decorator Showcase 2002

The blue and white color scheme of this sitting room was meant to echo the water, clouds, and sky visible in the third floor window view of the San Francisco Bay and the Golden Gate Bridge. The designer's mix of materials and styles adds dimension and interest to the space, especially the brightly colored piscine table legs.

Subtle Drama
Carol A. Jackson Interiors, Inc.
Charleston Symphony Orchestra League/ASID
Designers' Show House 2003

Inspiration for this room came from European grand homes, mansions, and palaces, where light is reflected off wall surfaces to counteract the dark, dreary winters. A silvery glaze was added to the walls of this music room to achieve the effect, completed with the use of mirrors and bright artwork. Lined silk panels were used to frame the windows, at subtle same time adding luxury and fullness to the room.

Nature's Sparkle
Stacey Lapuk Interior Design, Inc.
Marin Designers Showcase 2001

©John Sutton Photography

©John Sutton Photography

©John Sutton Photography

Drawing on the Romantic Movement's passion for nature, this room was made airy, garden-like, and fresh. The concept of flowers and leaves is repeated throughout the room, from the window sheers, to the ceiling border, the cabinetry detail, and the area rug. Silver and gold add metallic tingle to the room's green tinge.

Oui! Oui!
Karen L. Byrne
Vassar Show House 1999

©John Lewis Photography

Authentic French furnishings were used to create this classic parlor scene, focused on a fantastic fireplace surround. The oversize mirror makes the room feel even bigger than its generous proportions.

The Getaway
Carolyn Platt Antiques, Paoli Fabric
Vassar Show House 2001

©John Lewis Photography

Wonderfully restored antiques are more than showpieces in this room. Luxurious upholstery offers up comfort, amidst the rich green surround of papered walls.

Green with Beauty
Gary Roeberg Designer
Vassar Show House 2000

©John Lewis Photography

A palette of green and cream work together for tropical flair. Pinstripes enhance the elaborate architectural molding, drawing attention to the rich layers of care and effort that went into this duo-tone space.

Family Living Room
Miller Stein
ASID California Peninsula Chapter Designer
Showcase House 2003

davidduncanlivingston.com

Elegance and comfort unite in this luxurious family room, where practical and comfortable furniture makes for easy family living. The space maintains a light and airy nature through the use of garden colors, especially the sage-colored gauzy drapes, which bring the garden indoors.

The Glow of the Daystar
Lycknell Interiors
Vassar Show House 2001

The day doesn't have to invite the sun in, it's already there in a sunny yellow paneled wall. Soft colors combine for a soft, inviting environment in a secluded sitting room. A repeating motif of squares and rectangles enhances the unity achieved through color.

The Niche
Goldthorpe & Edwards,
Interior Design & Decoration
Vassar Show House 2001

Gold and pewter tones work together in gilded wallpaper, a floor with inset medallions, sparkling fringe, and a crystal chandelier. The royal effect would feel at home in Versailles.

Coming Home to the Woods
Ethan Allen Interiors
Vassar Show House 2001

The comfort of a tufted sofa and corner chaise act as lures to this richly accessorized, neoclassic living room.

An Artist's Haven
Miho Kahn Interiors
Vassar Show House 2002

Warm Mix
Cynthia Cericola-Hartz Interiors
Vassar Show House 2000

A multi-layered mix of rich, warm colors, luxurious textures, and eye-catching details establish the provincial French ambience in this inviting, versatile room. Comfortable furniture and personal treasures complete the mix, providing a harmonious and cozy gathering spot for family members and guests.

An old bed becomes a sofa table, discarded windows are transformed into a one-of-a-kind cabinet. The result is a stunning blend of elegance and practicality, a place filled with beauty that inspires and delights.

Homage to the Past
Cox Interior Design
Vassar Show House 2001

The influences of many popular revival styles were intermixed for a colorful blend of patterns, colors, and textures presented in a fresh, updated way.

The English Countryside
Hilary Musser Interior Design
Vassar Show House 2002

A wall mural and trompe l'oeil ceiling contribute to the rich warmth of this room. The effect of painting and rich fabrics combine for a long-lived in, mannerly feel.

Living Room
Charleston Design Center
Charleston Symphony Orchestra League/ASID
Designers' Show House 2002

Metallic bronzes and silvers combine with shades of cream and eggplant to create a dramatic color palette for this striking living room. The eclectic use of furniture adds to the elegance of the room, as do the sheers, silks, and taffetas that fill it.

Exotic Influence
Sonja Willman Designs
St. Louis Association of Realtors Designers'
Show House 2001

This room showcases a collector's favorite pieces. A
collection of ironstone plates hangs on the wall of an
arched inset. Asian antiques and modern fabrics round
out the look for an eclectic, harmonious balance.

Den/Sitting Room
Stan Kelly Interiors, Inc.
Center for Family Development
Designers' Showcase 2001

The designer brings his 18th and 19th century neoclassic styling to this room with a neutral palette that allows focus to remain on the antique furnishings and accessories. A 19th century down chaise lounge, oval English table, and a pair of custom-designed leather ottomans demonstrate an incredible sense of style through the combination of family heirlooms and newly designed items.

©2002 Celia Pearson/Pearson Photography

Guest Sitting Room
Stan Kelly Interiors, Inc.
National Symphony Orchestra Decorators' Show House 2001

Photography by Gordon Beall

A custom-designed iron and glass coffee table and a pair of chairs take center stage in a room where less is more. A monochromatic color scheme carries from the sisal floor covering to the drapery fabric. The designer even hand-painted the book covers that fill the walled bookcase in order to maintain the room's color palette.

An exquisitely carved Greek revival fireplace beckons to guests and family members while majestic windows dramatically frame the views of the lush terraced gardens. Wall coverings inspired by Shagreen from the past embellish the walls, and international accessories create peaceful harmony. The eclectic ambiance created here exudes pure elegance and sophistication. Truly, this Grand Salon is an interior to be enjoyed by all.

Servants' Quarters
Sonja Willman Designs
St. Louis Symphony Show
House & Gardens 2001

Brown stripes and earthy
textures dominate this room,
rich in style and comfort. Even
the master wouldn't mind
kicking his feet up here.

Alise O'Brien Architectural Photography

Alise O'Brien Architectural Photography

Lady's Retreat
Valentine Interiors Design & Decorating Shop
Shoreline Foundation Decorators'
Show House 2002

©Olson Photographic, LLC

Coated vinyl on the walls and the plush custom upholsteries and window treatments work to create a comforting, personal retreat for the lady of the house. The seating is intimate in scale, reflecting the nature of this privileged room. On the other hand, the windows are widened in effect with broad floor-to-ceiling drapery.

Music Parlor
Group3
Beaufort Academy Designer Show House 2000

The historically designed music parlor harmoniously blends together past and present to produce a luxurious space. Layers of silks and chenille, and a color palette of gold, black, muted greens, and natural hues make for an inviting, sensual experience.

Photography by Roger Squires

Seasoned Warmth
Amy B. Severin Design, Tracey Robb Interiors
Vassar Show House 2003

Three doors made this room feel more like a passage than the center of the home it deserved to be. To make it more of a stopping point, the designers decided to emphasize antique furnishings and textiles in a room dominated by fireplace and mantel. The strong architectural details were softened using elements reminiscent of nature.

Time in Art Deco
Justine Sancho Interior Design
National Symphony Orchestra Decorators' Show House 1999

Time moves backwards and forwards all at once in this room, distinguished by the Art Deco-inspired clock mural on the ceiling and fireplace wall. Period Art Deco accents, including clocks, Clarice Cliff pottery, and Bakelite accessories are complemented by contemporary furnishings with an Art Deco flavor. A custom-made rug was made especially to fit the atypical shape of the room, and to offset the strong colors of the mural above.

Panel of Experts
Lisa Newman Interiors
Shoreline Foundation
Decorators' Show House 2002

Using an old library globe as inspiration for the
textures and color palette, the designer used old
world architectural elements and contrasted them
with simple, clean, classic contemporary lines in the
furniture. Decorative painter Marc Potocsky put his
decorative painting skills to work to create the
impression that all the woodwork (new pine) in the
room was the same as that in the 100-year-old
fireplace that was salvaged from a nearby mansion
and installed in this house. Tromp l'oiel adds
additional detail, in faux dental molding and in the
diamond motif.

Keeping it Personal
Susan Dearborn Interiors, Inc.
Newport Show House Guild 2003

An understated room filled with personal memorabilia for added warmth is a place to relax, write, read, and entertain friends. The color palette takes its cue from the bird-themed carpet's blend of soft greens, persimmons, and beiges.

Conversation Retreat
Karen Brown Interiors, Inc.
Florida Orchestra Guild, St. Petersburg
Designer's Showcase 2002

The art of conversation is gilded, set in deep tones of sueded cocoa, subtle animal prints, and natural grass cloth. The result is a textural backdrop for the global mix of antique and new furnishings hailing from Europe, Africa, Bali, the Orient, and beyond. A telephone alcove at the rear offers a comfy upholstered bench with its super serving of privacy.

Rio Constantini Photography

The designers chose an affluent connoisseur of adventure and travel to be the occupant of this formal family room. Ruby, sage, gold, and ebony color the serene environment, where the excitement of the exotic and the comforts of home meet to create a space that would keep any traveler at home.

Tea by Design
Margery Wedderburn Interiors
Fall Design House at the Washington Design Center 2003

This sublevel basement room posed several challenges for the designer. With no natural lighting, she used blue lights and fake foliage behind windows to give the impression of an aboveground space. Also, by adding molding trim to the ceiling and faux painting the space in between the crown molding and the trim, the designer gave the illusion of more height to the space. Bamboo hardwood floors, natural sea grass woven wallcovering, and a constellation mirror add sleek and comfortable styling to the tranquil retreat.

Living Room
Your Space, Inc.
San Francisco Decorator Showcase 2003

Natural found objects such as rocks, kelp, and driftwood were used to create the "beach debris" theme for this living room. A dove gray palette with yellow accents lends a crisp and clean feeling to the space. The walls were upholstered in custom-printed Italian linen to match the upholstered furniture.

Half Twist
Exquisite Designs and Décor
The Loudoun Arts Council's
Designer Show House

A family room dares to be a little contemporary, with purple furnishings and drapes, an oversized clock, and a repeating half-oval motif.

Bright Impression
Interior Expressions
The Loudoun Arts Council's
Designer Show House

Continental Sitting Room
Stan Kelly Interiors, Inc.
Center for Family Development
Designers' Showcase 2003

A living room stretches off the foyer, providing an inspiring first for the home. Sunny yellow and garden green team up to form a background for artwork. The space is illuminated by a chandelier and pocket lights, set within a hand-painted ceiling medallion.

The juxtaposition of new and old elements creates a sense of drama in this highly stylized sitting room. The 19th century sofa and moderns tables demand attention in a room dominated by neutral tones, while the patterned drapes add interest and warmth.

Zen Modern
Rozalynn Woods Interior Design
ASID Pasadena Home Tour 2003

Photography by Peter Christiansen Valli

Photography by Peter Christiansen Valli

Photography by Peter Christiansen Valli

Photography by Peter Christiansen Valli

This Japanese-inspired home is a study in wholeness through simplicity and symmetry. The room is light and open, with crisp lines and soft furnishings. Clean and open, the space maintains an intimate quality.

Classic Comfort
John Cole Interior Design
Pasadena Showcase House 2003

This family room and adjacent terrace maintain the traditional styling set by the home's architectural features, yet exhibit a sense of human comfort. A custom-carved stone mantle corresponds to the terrace's fireplace. Inside, overscaled upholstery, unique iron lighting fixtures, masculine furnishings, and a custom area rug create an atmosphere of casual elegance. Hand-painted embellishments emphasize the room's coffered ceiling.

A Tropical Complement
DesignWorks Creative Partnership, Ltd.
American Lung Association of Florida
Designer Showhouse 2003

The designer decided to use a neutral color palette in this room so as not to compete with the abundant landscaping visible from the large windows. The choice provided suitable styling for the tropical environment while blending the exterior colors with the interior.

Contemporary Classic Living Room
Justine Sancho Interior Design
Washington Design Center Architectural Digest
Private Rooms of Washington 2000

Casual elegance and sophistication breeze into this room through the use of old world antiques and contemporary furnishings in a soft palette of greens and melons. Silk fabrics enhance the look achieved with the antique limestone fireplace and Jerusalem limestone flooring.

English Tudor with a Cosmopolitan Twist
John Cole Interior Design
Pasadena Showcase House 1999

Photography by Martin Fine

A massive living room was sectioned into four areas in order to maintain a sense of warmth and intimacy. Utilizing an array of complimentary fabrics, the designer also managed to make the space feel friendlier, without sacrificing elegance or sophistication. Collected accessories from around the globe give this English room an exciting cosmopolitan twist.

Photography by Martin Fine

Photography by Martin Fine

A Bold Statement
P & H Interiors Inc.
American Lung Association of Florida
Designer Showhouse 2003

Custom-made furnishings, bold faux finishes, and strong colors create a room that is rich in elegance and warmth. The room supports the designer's philosophy that people need comfort and aesthetics in their interior spaces.

CHAPTER 3
LIBRARIES, STUDIES, AND HOME OFFICES

Study for a Francophile
Penelope Rozis
San Francisco Decorator Show
House 2000

With only one tiny window, the designer felt this room was in need of a view. She created one by using six-foot high vignettes of Paris by Fred Lyon. The galvanized top table desk with polished brass edge detail is reminiscent of zinc bars. Toile-covered bergere chairs add a traditional touch to this modern interior.

Blues in Black and White
Lisa Newman Interiors
Middlesex County YMCA,
Lyman Homestead Showhouse

Splashes of fuchsia punctuate this feminine sanctuary, which boasts a fresh, complex color palette. The wall color "reminded me of a Tiffany gift box," says the designer, equating the effect with "the gold standard of luxury" and "treating yourself well." Set aside as a lady's retreat, the space affords three resting spots where she can gather her thoughts, write them all down, or toss them in the fire.

Anne Gummerson Photography

Ultrasuede Investigation
Anne Markstein Interiors
Baltimore Symphony Associates
Decorators' Show House 2001

Anne Gummerson Photography

Ultrasuede paneling installed on the walls
and the luxuriously soft armchairs add
texture to the smooth finish of this
modern library. A contemporary craft
collection and custom-made writing desk
and rug give character to the sleek and
comfortable room.

A Study in Transition
Bruce Norman Long Interior Design
Kips Bay Showhouse 2002

A large landing hall between two bedrooms was transformed into an inviting study area. A modern steel surround fireplace complements the custom-made aluminum lacquered desk. A deep chaise upholstered in silk velvet adds texture to the space, while flat white walls and moldings and espresso-colored mahogany floors add to the juxtaposition of modern and traditional styling.

©image/dennis krukowski

©image/dennis krukowski

Work of Art
Personal Style, LLC, and Office Furniture USA,
a Division of Fuller Office Furniture
Shoreline Foundation Decorators' Show House 1999

Photography by Michael Partenio Productions, Danbury, CT

Photography by Michael Partenio Productions, Danbury, CT

Photography by Michael Partenio Productions, Danbury, CT

Instead of mismatched hand-me-downs, this home office boasts sleek custom-designed furniture, upholstered walls, stainless-steel window treatments, and original artwork. Stunning architectural photography and 3D works of art make the office chores more entertaining in this fabulous, golden-tone space.

Clean Reading
Teal Michel, ASID
Rock Hill Women's Club Designer Show House

To maximize the outdoor views in this library, the designer chose a color palette that included greens, blues, and creams. At the homeowner's request, the two original bookcases and curved recessed window cornices were kept, while an unsightly radiator was hidden by the construction of a window ledge. The designer used two 19th century Chinese Temple Carvings to decorate the ledge's front panels and to break the run of the cabinetry.

A Room of Your Own
Elisabeth A. Lane
Vassar Show House 2002

A light and cheery room is a respite for the lady of the house. Located in a nook off the master bedroom, it is a space set aside for reading, writing, and other projects.

Le Salon de la Femme
The French Lemon
Vassar Show House 2002

A woman's home office is tastefully attired in French style, and set against sunny yellow wall stripes.

A Sabbatical from the Ordinary
Toby Strogatz Interiors at Xcessories
Vassar Show House 2002

Designed as a retreat, one enters from a delicately decorated hallway to a wimply furnished room rich with sensuous fabrics and textures.

Studious Nature
Kelley Interior Design Service
Traditional Design House at the
Washington Design Center 2002

Greetings from the Home Office
Faith Ashley Interiors
Tara Drive Decorator Showhouse 2003

Dramatic contrasts of light and dark emphasize the room's role as a place for pensive study. The lighting is striking, without being overpowering, the furnishings classic and comfortable, and the overall effect quite magnificent.

The designer found her inspiration for this space in the Southern Plantation style homes built in the United States during the 19th and 20th centuries, however the room also features influences from Colonial, English and Caribbean styles as well. The use of rich woods, primarily mahogany balanced with the dark brown trim and light cane colored Venetian plastered walls, gives the room a handsome yet calming effect. The U-shaped 19th Century Planter's Desk is the centerpiece for this space, with it's unique shape and finely carved legs and leather top. Finishing off the room are the beautiful silk drapery panels, hand-carved mahogany leaf fan, the English game chairs, and the Tommy Bahama sitting chair. The pineapple emblem, which is the international welcome symbol, has been used throughout the room.

Serious Study
Cinda Vote Design Group
Evansville Living Idea Home 2003

Bryan Leazenby/OnSite Images for Evansville Living Magazine

Bryan Leazenby/OnSite Images for Evansville Living Magazine

An asymmetrical swag drape complements the old world elegance and earthy, masculine tones that dominate this eclectic interior. A cashmere shawl was the designer's inspiration for the room, its paisley design found in pillow accents, the swag, and a cozy chair.

Bryan Leazenby/OnSite Images for Evansville Living Magazine

Bryan Leazenby/OnSite Images for Evansville Living Magazine

73

Earthy Wisdom
Richar Interiors Inc.
Chicago Home and Garden Design House 2003

Photography by David Schilling

This library embodies rustic charm with its hand-hewn hickory plank flooring, distressed wood finishes, and rich textures in warm tones like terracotta and soft green. The designer achieves an overall look full of aged elegance and earthy sensibility.

Photography by David Schilling

Old World Reference
John Cole Interior Design
Pasadena Showcase House 2002

This library exudes a stately air with its mahogany-paneled walls, antique French Louis XIV walnut stretcher base table, and English bachelor chest. Fine furnishings were upholstered in floral, paisley, and plaid patterns. Leather-bound books and old world prints help complete the look.

For an English Bibliophile
Patricia McLean Interiors, Inc.
Atlanta Symphony Orchestra
Decorators' Show House 1999

Photography by Robert Thein

This paneled library, with a Gringling Gibbons style fireplace and bay window surrounded by tall bookcases, is the heart of the home. An antique Oushak rug vibrant in terra cottas, creams, and golds, is the anchor for a warm chinoiserie linen combined with a crisp taffeta stripe and passementerie that frame the window. English caned library chairs, club chairs, and leather club fender provide ample seating for important meetings or just relaxing with a book.

The Professional Woman
Karen Brown Interiors, Inc.
Sarasota ASID Designer Showhouse 2000

An elegantly appointed home office is a must for today's busy woman executive. Faux leather panels in warm caramel and rich khaki paint treatment touched with gold provide a backdrop that is femininely sophisticated without being frilly. Fabric wrapped panels, painted woodwork, and crown moulding soften the room and provide interest. Thoughtfully chosen antique accessories and artwork complete the look in this home office, which is strong enough for a man, but made for a woman.

Robert Crum Photography

Liberated Library
Bergeson Design Studio, LLC
Loudoun Art Council's Designer Showhouse 2003

Usually the library is treated as a masculine space, but this time the designer wanted to turn that around. She wanted a soft look, envisioning a client who has traveled a great deal, has many interests, and writes poetry. Working with a pallete of worn, warm celadon introduced a feeling pf timelessness to this brand-new home. Medallions hand-finished by the designer and applied to the crown molding create an additional detail with posts added to the medallions at strategic spots to use as drapery hangers. The "coffered" ceiling is really a tromp l'leil created by the faux finisher at the request of the designer to add to the feeling of a timeless space.

Working Woman en Suite
Lark Interiors, CMD Interiors
Vassar Show House 2001

Whether running a household, organizing fundraisers, or working at home, every woman needs her special place to work and plan.

Poetic Haven Room and Bathroom
SJ Designs, Flair Design Group,
and Maisel Interiors
ASID California Peninsula Chapter
Designer Showcase House 2003

Antiques and modern reproductions were used in conjunction with today's classic silk fabrics to achieve the look of old world elegance. Any romantic poet would feel at home in this petite chamber, its color scheme of pale peach, gold, and sage repeated in the bathroom. Hand-painted, faux-finished, stenciled walls tie into the designs of the Asmara Aubusson rug. The Narcissus Silk Taffeta Grand Canape, antique Kingwood writing desk, and antique bibliotheque are timeless.

Photography by Norbert von der Groeben

Reading Sanctuary
Bernadette V. Upton Interior Design
American Lung Association of Florida Designer
Showhouse 2003

©2003 Robert Ludwick 954-785-9919

Delve into treasured books among tactile touches of velvet stretched over a plush sofa. An alluring palette of copper, corals, browns, and mellow yellows entices you into the comforts of this sensuous room. Chinoiserie furnishings were used to add spice, while the library walls were upholstered to soften and enhance the wood.

CHAPTER 4
DINING ROOMS AND BREAKFAST NOOKS

Gordon Beall Photography

Renaissance Appeal
Justine Sancho Interior Design
National Symphony Orchestra
Decorators' Show House 2000

Gordon Beall Photography

Classic blends with contemporary for a luxurious and light
atmosphere. The designer integrated contemporary seating with
antiques and reproductions. Sepia-toned drawings of Renaissance
botanical prints cover the wall, adding to the sense of aged
refinement. Rich and regal, the dining room sets an inviting tone.

Photography by Christopher Dow

Garden Delight
John Cole Interior Design
Pasadena Showcase House 2001

Photography by Christopher Dow

Taking its cue from the garden outside, this room
boasts loads of texture, color, and patterns. Botanical
prints on the walls, a hand-painted organic trellis,
and floral print upholstery complete the look.

Exotic Cuisine
Marshal Field's Interior Design Studio
Junior League of Detroit
Designers' Show House 2002

Classically detailed moldings, fine Chinese antiques, silk upholstered walls, and glittering tabletop accessories come together to form a room rich in luxury. Textures in a palette composed of Chinese persimmon, Canton cobalt, and fresh Empire green make for an exciting and intriguing dining experience.

Family Feeling
Lisa Davenport's Home Gallery
Shoreline Foundation
Decorators' Show House 2002

This dining room is elegantly set with Grandma's antique china, stressing comfort and the importance of assembled friends and family. Upholstered walls, a Swarovski crystal chandelier, and silk draperies surround the medley of English and Italian furniture.

In a Country Manor
John Cole Interior Design
Assistance League of Southern
California Design House 2001

Photography by Peter Christiansen Valli

Photography by Peter Christiansen Valli

A coral, green, and cream palette add
casual elegance to this grand dining room.
Flowers bloom in upholstery,
wallcoverings, above glass cabinets, and on
the table to create a fresh approach and
bring life to the room.

©John Lewis Photography

©John Lewis Photography

Layers of coral, distinctive greens, and ivories serve to enhance the "sable" foundation used to highlight intricate Adam-esque details in this luxurious dining room. Authentic, circa 1785 Jean-Baptiste Reveillon polychrome hand-printed panels were selected to accentuate the architectural millwork.

Savor the Elegance
Light-Parker Galleries
Vassar Show House 2002

Bursts of color punctuate a room sumptuously adorned in timelessly elegant furnishings.

Dorian Graye's Tender Gaze
Knowlton Associates, LLC
Lourdes Show House 2003

Formal and elegant styling with gold accents defines this dining experience. Hand-painted French chairs are upholstered in an array of brilliant colors, including cobalt blue, bright pink, lime green, and yellow.

A Secluded Garden Party
Patricia McLean Interiors, Inc.
Atlanta Symphony Orchestra
Decorators' Show House 2000

Hand-painted Gracie panels customized in Hong Kong set the stage for a charming dining experience. Yellow, peach, and terra cotta flowers among the green grasses and trees span the garden wall. The mood is formal, yet fun-loving, with two round Regency style tables to provide plenty of seating for guests.

A Place to Gather
Carol A. Jackson Interiors, Inc.
Charleston Symphony Orchestra League/ASID Designers' Show House 2001

Cheerful bright yellow walls and a faux-coppered ceiling set the stage for old world furnishings and an Italian style fireplace. The warm tone fabrics come from the chosen pear motif used throughout the room. This space was designed to welcome, comfort, and energize all that gather here.

Roman Dining Atrium
Teal Michel, ASID and Creative
Design Solutions, Inc.
Charlotte Symphony Guild
ASID Show House 2001

Photography by Doug Palmer

This formal dining room was designed to serve as a daily destination and peaceful retreat. Glass-top wicker tables balance the grandiose and dramatic Roman colonnade, which received a special silver finish to give the appearance of marble. Lush greenery and a water fountain bring the outdoors in.

Photography by Doug Palmer

New Age Dining Meets "This Old House"
Pauline Vastardis Interiors
Vassar Show House 2001

©John Lewis Photography

An eclectic blend of Asian, contemporary, and traditional influences were used to blend the grace of a previous century with the simplicity of today.

Photography by Stewart O'Shields

Fine Dining
Bruce Norman Long Interior Design
Princeton Junior League Show House 2000

Photography by Stewart O'Shields

This dining room's original oak paneled walls, plaster strap work ceiling, and stone cased leaded windows and doors provided a good base from which this design team could work. The enormous scale of the room allowed for the use of four custom-made leather tables with mirrored tops surrounded by sixteen chairs that were painted in a Venetian coral color with gilded accents and upholstered in a Fortuny style fabric.

89

Naturally Different
Richar Interiors Inc.
Chicago Home and Garden
Design House 2003

In shades of green and shrimp, the designer envisioned the dining room rich in natural hues and ambient lighting. Nature is evoked throughout the room with references to the garden – a latticework hanging lantern, floral themes, and a table constructed of planked marquetry top supported by a carved stone base.

Photography by David Schilling

Eclect-fast Room
Lisa Newman Interiors
Newport Show House Guild, 2003

©Olson Photographic, LLC

The family's command center includes an unexpected blend of color and elements. Child friendly with faux leather chairs and a patterned vintage rug, it still maintains its sense of style.

New Wave
Lisa Newman Interiors
WBNA Povidence Design House 2003

©Olson Photographic, LLC

©Olson Photographic, LLC

A cross-cultural space weds the clean lines of classic contemporary furnishings to an organic backdrop of Asian undertones. Inspired by a famous woodblock print by Japanese artist Katsusjika Hokusai, the designer herself painted the wave mural and glass artist Ray Mathews created the unique lighting fixture. The complex color palette rises from the depths of the sea to finish with the silvery sparkle of ocean spray.

Alan Goldstein Photography / Courtesy of Van Metre Homes

Party of Great
J & L Interiors
The Loudoun Arts Council's
Designer Show House

Purple and gold team up with green accents for an elegant atmosphere perfect for dinner parties. Artwork, upholstery, and even the table settings enhance the sophisticated, romantic theme.

Traditional elements meet a fresh and sophisticated approach. French brushed walls are the backdrop for antique country chairs. Toile and checked fabric frame the doorway and upholster the chairs. An oval table skirted in Matelesse over black file holds black and white china and all the accoutrements for a successful lunch.

Photography by Pat Shanklin

Photography by Pat Shanklin

A Light Meal
Evaline Karges Interiors
Evansville Living Idea Home 2003

Centering their design around the bright and cheery wallpaper, the designers created a traditional, yet light and airy space. An antique crystal chandelier hangs above an English reproduction pedestal table surrounded by painted Chinese Chippendale chairs. The round table adds interest to the square room.

Bryan Leazenby/OnSite Images for Evansville Living Magazine

Bryan Leazenby/OnSite Images for Evansville Living Magazine

Bryan Leazenby/OnSite Images for Evansville Living Magazine

93

Imperial Palm Beach
Ayres Bartholomew Interiors,
Dakota Wall Arts
American Lung Association of Florida
Designer Showhouse 2003

Inspiration for this dining room came from its grand scale and the spectacular view from the arched window. Oversized pieces including a French tapestry and Louis XV mirror help to fill up the expansive space and add to the ambiance. Furnishings include a mahogany table with tripod drum base made of mixed wood veneers and a marquetry top, dining table in classical mahogany Provincial style with a stone parquet top. The walls were hand-stenciled to give the appearance of age, and the tromp l'oleil molding adds dimension to the walls.

Good Morning Sunshine
Kelley Interior Design Service, Inc.
Center for Family Development
Designers' Showcase 2003

Bright, sunny light never leaves this breakfast nook, drenched in crisp whites and yellows. Sunflower print panels frame the window and are punctuated by accents of black throughout the room.

Dinner with the Duchess
Taylor Wells Design
Baltimore Symphony Associates
Decorators' Show House 2000

The designer wanted to create a room that was historically accurate and formal, yet related to the natural landscape that surrounded the historic home where Wallace Simpson, the Duchess of Windsor, spent her summers. The wallpaper, which shows a French hunt scene, was recreated from a 19th century original. The three-part mahogany dining table and sideboard are period originals, while the other furnishings and accessories are reproductions of period pieces. Overall, the room provides a fresh and refined dining atmosphere.

CHAPTER 5
KITCHENS

Country/Old World Fusion
Helen Marshburn, Koehler
Kitchen and Bath
Classic American Homes Show House 2000

Courtesy of Wood-Mode/Photography by The Shadowlight Group

Courtesy of Wood-Mode/Photography by The Shadowlight Group

Courtesy of Wood-Mode/Photography by The Shadowlight Group

American country and old world styling come together to form a cozy, relaxed, and attractive combination. Red accents in an otherwise neutral palette add to the kitchen's warmth and appeal.

Courtesy of Wood-Mode

The kitchen's brown and yellow backsplash adds excitement to this traditionally styled space.
Red and yellow are repeated in the kitchen's light fixture and center island, spreading color
throughout. The special hood features decorative molding and resembles stone for an aged look.

Courtesy of Wood-Mode

Courtesy of Wood-Mode

Contrast in the Kitchen
Richar Interiors Inc.
Chicago Home and Garden
Design House 2003

Old world styling promotes a casual atmosphere in this kitchen dominated by cabinets. A cantaloupe wall frames the large window for a striking effect. Light and dark contrasts are maintained throughout the room with pine cabinets and dark stained fir. Hammered sterling silver sinks and pillowed marble stone backsplash add warmth and special character.

Photography by David Schilling

Tuscan Appeal
Karen Padgett Prewitt
Charleston Symphony Orchestra League/ASID
Designers' Show House 2001

Rick Rhodes Photography

www.trippsmithphotography.com

www.trippsmithphotography.com

Old world elements like Tuscan columns and acanthus leaf border tiles combined with state of the art fittings create a beautiful kitchen. A light limestone floor makes the space seem bigger and defines the dark island. A plaid silk taffeta window treatment was chosen to complement the granite countertops and backsplashes. Parchment faux-finished walls are reminiscent of yellow ocher walls in Tuscan villas aged by years of cooking fires.

Carmine's Cucina
Morris Black Designs Studios
Vassar Show House 2000

Formal elegance and sleek function combine for a timeless kitchen. Buttery yellow cabinetry, subtly distressed, stands in dynamic counterpoint to state-of-the-art stainless appliances.

Old English Country Kitchen
The Rutt Studio on the Main Line
Vassar Show House 2001

Freestanding pieces of furniture and an emphasis on the stove hood lend themselves to the authenticity of an Old English country kitchen. Special mullion glass doors and antique details work with a café latte color palette.

Tuscan Autumn
Style House
Vassar Show House 2001

Drawing on Tuscany, this galley kitchen area contrasts an expanse of working white sink with rich wood tones and gold paint with a patina finish.

©John Lewis Photography

Just a Taste
The Rutt Studio on the Main Line
Vassar Showhouse 2002

Old-Time Style
Nesting Feathers, Inc.
Vassar Show House 2002

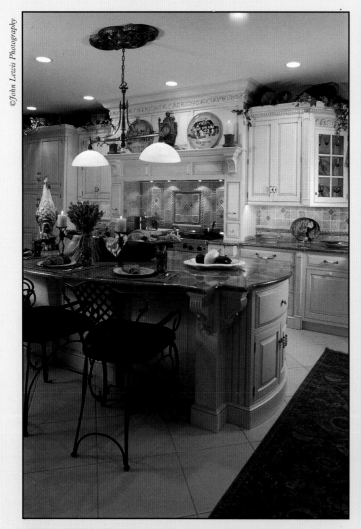

©John Lewis Photography

©John Lewis Photography

Glazed cabinetry, rich terra cotta colored granite, antiqued copper fixtures, and warm chutney woods were carefully selected to evoke a sun-drenched day in an Italian villa. Careful attention to the fine details of handcrafted furniture were delicately woven into the design.

Carved details on the cabinets and the warm, rich tones of wooden flooring give the impression of age in a contemporary kitchen. Details on the ceiling add comfort to the space, where hours could be spent enjoying the smells and the sights.

Double Islands
Design Galleria Kitchen & Bath Studio
Alliance Children's Theatre Guild Christmas House 2002

A large hood is the focal point of this soaring space. The hood caps a state-of-the-art cook center, and overlooks two islands and the finest appliances money can buy. Double ovens and a pullout pantry are disguised in a stained armoire to the right of the hood, and matching distressed cabinetry conceals the Sub-Zero refrigerator. Black granite countertops, dark wood floors, and marble backsplashes blend perfectly with the other finishes in the room, and textured fabrics appear throughout the space in warm shades of brown, cream, black, and red.

Photography by Kevin Rose/Atlanta

Photography by Kevin Rose/Atlanta

Photography by Kevin Rose/Atlanta

Photography by Kevin Rose/Atlanta

Classic Vintage
Peter Dunham, Rick and Debbie Nasetta, CKD, CBD
House Beautiful Celebrity Showhouse 2002

Style and comfort go hand in hand in this kitchen, with cabinetry in Antique white and an island in a custom red vintage finish. Charcoal gray soapstone used for the countertops adds to the room's vintage quality, while the white farmhouse sink with polished nickel hardware completes the look.

Stone on the Range
Design Galleria Kitchen & Bath Studio
Atlanta Symphony Orchestra
Decorators' Show House 2001

Photography by David Schilling/Atlanta

Photography by David Schilling/Atlanta

Fine detailing, furniture elements, sophisticated finishes and the latest in interior cabinet accessories make this kitchen an integral par t of the home. This bold room also features stone floors and walls, with a focal cherry-paneled stove hood over the 48-inch professional range.

A Real Pearl
Design Galleria Kitchen & Bath Studio
Junior League of Nashville, Decorators'
Show House 2000

Photography by David Schlling/Atlanta

Photography by David Schlling/Atlanta

Unique architecture and an eclectic former owner (Minnie Pearl) inspired the design for this charming kitchen. The space is centered on a round, tile-topped table island, which provides extra workspace as well as seating. The shape of the table is repeated in the subtle curve of the cabinetry facing. Distressed finishes perpetuate the ambiance, along with delicious colors, pleasing textures, and state-of-the-art appliances.

Photography by David Schlling/Atlanta

Courtesy of Wood-Mode/Photography by BRT Photographic Illustrations

In a Silent Way
Victoria Hagen
Town and Country
Show House 2002-2003

Courtesy of Wood-Mode/Photography by BRT Photographic Illustrations

White wood paneling dominates this kitchen, where class and comfort combine to form an appealing space. Stainless steel appliances and light fixtures add a modern flair to the classic country styling, and the light-rich windows seem to say, "Stay here a while."

Universal Design
Dan Parks and John Kelly
Universal Design Demonstration Home 2002

In a home designed for people with special needs – like those with limited movement, confined to a wheelchair, or elderly populations. The challenge was to create an attractive design in conjunction with universal design principles. The designers kept with the architectural theme of an upscale early twentieth century shingle-style beach house, and used special Wood-Mode cabinetry with special adjustable components, including an electronically operated sink that moved closer to the ground for easier operation and accessibility.

Outside-In
Karen Padgett Prewitt
Beaufort Academy
Designer Show House 2003

The view of majestic old oaks and a river framed by the kitchen windows was the inspiration for this kitchen's color scheme. The designer chose to bring the outdoors inside, and painted dated cabinets the gray-green color of Spanish moss. Mellow old Savannah-gray brick anchors a working island that separates the kitchen from what was once a screened porch.

A Residential Approach
Susan Fredman & Associates, Ltd.
Lake Forest Showcase House 2003

George Lambros Photography

The designer transformed a commercial kitchen into a residential one by painting the original cabinets a soft cream in order to serve as a backdrop to the recently refurbished original stainless steel sink and countertops. A honed mocha marble tile was used to add richness to the room. A sage green, olive, rust, red, and cream color palette creates a vintage look, which is made complete by the combination of old and new elements.

George Lambros Photography

Eating in Tandem
Lycknell Interiors
Vassar Show House 2003

Side-by-side dining area and kitchen were designed together, with warm wood tones tying them together thematically, along with period furnishings evocative of an era of family style meals, when the kitchen was the heart of the home.

Sleek and Chic
Joe Ruggiero and Pamela Baird, CKD
San Francisco Design Center Idea House 1999

Style and sophistication reign in this kitchen, where cooking happens fashionably. The eclectic blend of materials like stainless steel appliances, the shiny black island, wood and white cabinets, warehouse-like ceiling, and wooden floor coordinate magnificently for a hip and contemporary space.

Where the View is Clear
John A. Buscarello, ASID
Hudson River Designer Showhouse 2000

Cherry cabinets and stainless steel appliances compliment the extra-special countertop made of solidified volcanic ash.
Traditional-looking elements are blended with the modern to create an exciting space, worthy of the view from the windows.

Courtesy of Wood-Mode/©2000 Peter R. Peirce, Inc.   *Courtesy of Wood-Mode/©2000 Peter R. Peirce, Inc.*   *Courtesy of Wood-Mode/©2000 Peter R. Peirce, Inc.*

Rising Up
Design Galleria Kitchen & Bath Studio
Atlanta Symphony Orchestra Decorators' Show House 2000

©2000 David Schilling/Atlanta

A grand staircase and 22-foot ceiling set this kitchen above the rest. A neutral palette allows decorative elements such as the paneled range hood, beveled leaded-glass doors, and carved corbels to ornament the space, while varying cabinet heights and depths give the room a furnished look. A polished Italian chandelier shines o©2000 David Schilling/Atlantan the cobblestone floors, granite countertops, and brushed-nickel accessories. Pocket doors conceal and television set and countertop appliances, while a desk area disguises a computer station.

©2000 David Schilling/Atlanta

©2000 David Schilling/Atlanta

Beam There Before
B² Group, Nu-Way
Shoreline Foundation Decorators' Show House 2002

Little natural lighting was available for the work and breakfast nook areas of the kitchen. So the designers used a taupe glaze cabinet finish and limestone-colored floor tile to brighten the space. Charged with incorporating pre-existing mahogany beams, they tied the darker color in with the overall design through the central island area. Stainless steel appliances create a gourmet feeling within the old and comfortable atmosphere of the decor.

West Indies Meets Classic French Country
Roomscapes of Brevard
Brevard Symphony Orchestra's
Designer Show House 2000

Various work centers make for a beautiful and efficient space. Some special design features of this kitchen include the center island's warming drawer and cookware storage, two fully integrated dishwashers, a large mantle hood with pullout spice storage, and appliance garages along the cooking wall. Special carved wood moldings add elegance and character.

Courtesy of Wood-Mode

Courtesy of Wood-Mode

Taditional Twist
Pickens Homes, LLC
Evansville Living Idea Home 2003

Glazed pine custom-crafted cabinets are the main focus of the kitchen, covering almost every wall surface – including the dishwasher and refrigerator. A Heritage finish gives the cabinets a worn and distressed look, giving the kitchen an old world character. The kitchen sink looks old, but is made of Corian for easy maintenance. In the breakfast nook, a pine antique finish table complements the cabinetry.

What's New?
Kitchen and Bath Design Studio (Lorena Oden) and Peter Lauren Buckley, IFDA
Metropolitan Home Designer Showhouse at the Washington Design Center 2001

Courtesy of Wood-Mode

Courtesy of Wood-Mode

The designer envisioned a kitchen center for a large and busy family lifestyle, where serious cooking, entertaining, and relaxing could take place. Two separate islands make for practical and efficient maneuvering in the kitchen. Natural quartz and granite countertops also include a manmade stone, contributing color to the space, as do the glass-tile backsplashes with copper threads and beautiful Cider-toned cabinetry. A collection of watercolors and tall shutters soften and add warm to the space.

Courtesy of Wood-Mode

116

Contemporary Farmhouse Kitchen
Design Solutions, Inc.
Anne Arundel Medical Center Auxiliary
Designer Show House 2000

Photography by John Coyle Jr., Baltimore MD

Photography by John Coyle Jr., Baltimore MD

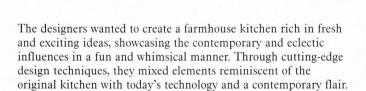

Photography by John Coyle Jr., Baltimore MD

The designers wanted to create a farmhouse kitchen rich in fresh
and exciting ideas, showcasing the contemporary and eclectic
influences in a fun and whimsical manner. Through cutting-edge
design techniques, they mixed elements reminiscent of the
original kitchen with today's technology and a contemporary flair.

Photography by John Coyle Jr., Baltimore MD

Layers of sunny color on the walls, and an antique green finish on the
moldings create a warm surround for a kitchen stocked with coppery hues.

CHAPTER 6
SUNROOMS AND PORCHES

Bird's-Eye View
Home & Garden Culture
Vassar Show House 2003

A tropical sunroom and bird aviary was transformed into a colorful paradise. A bevy of orchids in interesting containers, and other tropical plants bring the room to life. A slow-moving fan sets a pace for relaxation.

©John Lewis Photography

©Barry Halkin Photography, Philadelphia

Vaulted to the Top
Devine Designs, Inc.
Deborah Hospital Foundation
Show House 2001

A conservatory screams color, presenting an eye-popping mix of gold and scarlet from floor to the barrel-vaulted ceiling. The floor covering and furnishings are understated, with the exception of a central tablecloth, so as to allow the architecture to make its bold statement.

Breakfast in the Conservatory
Bloomingdale's, King of Prussia
Vassar Show House 2001

A sunroom was given a bright coat of paint and sunny, multi-patterned fabrics to create an environment perfect for the morning's first cup of coffee.

Room with a View
Pauline Vastardis Interiors
Vassar Show House 2000

A latticework of rose wallpaper crowns a bright sunroom, where comforting furnishings beckon in the reflected glory of the woods and garden beyond.

Weather the Weather
Kelley Interior Design Service, Inc.
National Symphony Orchestra
Decorators' Show House 2003

Bold and modern in black, white, and red, this porch makes for a stylish gathering place in all kinds of summer weather. Indoor/outdoor white fabric panels trimmed in black Velcro keep out the elements, while the furniture is weather-resistant, and the sisal flooring can't be damaged by moisture.

Photography by Ross Chapple

The Garden Room
Cynthia Cericola-Hartz Interiors
Vassar Show House 2002

©John Lewis Photography

Inspired by the indoor-outdoor way of life in southern France, the designer worked to incorporate the rich, warm hues of Provence in this elegant yet comfortable sunroom.

A Sunny Room
The Secret Garden
Evansville Living Idea Home 2003

Bryan Leazenby/OnSite Images for Evansville Living Magazine

Beautiful, custom-designed spider web grid patterned windows inspired the designers of this sunroom to bring the outdoors in. They achieved this by using only live plants for color and texture, and by incorporating accessories with a floral and dragonfly theme. Of particular interest in the room is the antique iron architectural piece that was transformed into a coffee table.

Bryan Leazenby/OnSite Images for Evansville Living Magazine

The Cottage Porch
Silver Moon Studio
Vassar Show House 2003

Hand-painted and hand-decorated murals of antique roses in full bloom capture a moment in time. Soft colors and time-aged furnishings relax the eye and allow feelings of tranquility and peacefulness to greet you in a European cottage-style entry porch.

Tea in the Garden
Cabbages & Roses LLC
The Loudoun Arts Council's
Designer Show House

A screened-in porch is themed for tea parties, with a collection of serving ware set amidst rose-patterned upholsteries.

Photography by E.A. Kennedy, III/Staff photographer Palm Beach Post

Alan Goldstein Photography/Courtesy of Van Metre Homes

Completely Overlooked
Susan Dearborn Interiors, Inc.
American Red Cross
Designer Show House 1999

The sophisticated whimsy of this balcony reflects an imaginary owner's love of modern sculpture and eclectic pieces from the Gasiunasen Gallery in Palm Beach, Florida. Adirondack chairs integrate North and South, while a canvas valence, draperies, and roll-up blinds proffer an opportunity to screen the room off and create a delightful enclosure for daytime reading or nighttime reflection.

American Glory
Knowlton Associates, LLC
Zurbrugg Lourdes Show House 2000

Situated on the Delaware River, overlooking a sailing club, a nautical all-American oasis theme was the obvious choice for this sunroom.

Space Illuminated
Plum Interior Design
Newport Show House 2003

The designer of this narrow porch wanted to transform the dark space into a light-filled haven that would soothe and refresh. To do this, she added mirrors to the wall facing the windows, and track lighting resembling candles to the ceiling, thus bringing the outdoors in and giving the space an ethereal quality. A faux-stone octagonal pedestal table, klismos-style chairs, and a classic-looking chaise furnish the room, which the designer has transformed into a special retreat.

CHAPTER 7
BEDROOMS

Sensual Palette
Stacey Lapuk Interior Design, Inc.
Marin Designers Showcase 2001

Trips to France and Costa Rica inspired this powerful color presentation. The effect of the honey, persimmon, and deep purple tones combine for sensual, relaxing effect. Ridges recur throughout as a design element, in the legs of the bed, the silver candle holders, the night tables, plant containers, and so on, carried throughout a complicated fusion of old and new international furnishings.

First Mate
BNK Design Consultants, Inc.
DOG HAUS – SPCA
Decorators' Show House 2003

A lush bedroom in sexy and classic styling features a canopy bed cloaked with ivory cashmere. The bed sits in front of a mirror-paneled wall, accompanied by two chairs and an ottoman covered in a black and white hound-tooth pattern, an elegant mahogany desk, two chic demilunes, and architectural accents like wood moldings and red walls.

©2002 Michael LoBiondo

A French bed awaits Madame or Mademoiselle in this penthouse chamber. Neutral walls with rouge stripes provide the perfect backdrop for rouge and cream checked bed hangings. Curtains of the same silk and sheer frame or conceal the view. With a nod to the contemporary setting, antiques and well-placed accessories complete the look of this charming room.

©2002 Michael LoBiondo

Stuck on You
Sonja Willman Designs
St. Louis Symphony
Show House and Gardens 2000

Red stucco walls characterize this bedroom and enhance its already cozy styling. Rich colors and textures provide a sense of warmth, while an eclectic blend of collectibles adds personality.

130

Retro Retreat
Avant Architects
ASID Omaha Symphony
Designer Show House 2003

Photography by Jeffrey Bebee

Retro styling of the loft is accompanied by a timeless feel. This bedroom was kept free of excessive ornamentation, save the custom-made green cloth headboard, swing-arm light fixtures, and hanging mobiles. To solve the problem of uneven light distribution due to the windows' placement, the designers used a unique mixture of stain and paint to lighten the originally dark trim. Blonde wood furniture was also used to help reflect light more evenly. The bathroom makes use of these same themes, with vibrant color and varied texture against a neutral palette.

Photography by Jeffrey Bebee

Oceanside Elegance
Wheeler Design Group
San Francisco Decorator Showcase 2003

An ocean-inspired color palette of blue, caramel and copper tones fills this guest bedroom, defined by its classic elegance. Fine antiques and modern furniture harmoniously balance with the understated finishes, fine fabrics, and timeless details to create a peaceful, ocean side retreat.

Still in There
Shelley Gordon Interior Design, Ltd.
Coyote Point Museum Auxiliary Decorator Show House

Taking its cue from the expansive views of the San Francisco Bay, this peaceful retreat reflects the natural environment with its soft sea green and neutral sea grass palette. Contrasting elements – modern furniture and traditional antiques, Asian and European objects, soft velvets and horsehair – provide balance, and achieve an overall feeling of peace and tranquility.

Fragrant Inspiration
Diane Hughes Interiors
Old York Historical Society
Decorator Show House 2003

One awakens luxuriously fresh in this master bedroom, where silks, elegant trims, and tassels contribute to a feeling of ageless beauty. A majestic four-poster bed takes center stage in the space, making room for a European inlay chest, English period bureau, and a large bay of windows. The seafoam, white, and ecru wallcovering ties everything together.

Age-Old Comfort
Sonja Willman Designs
St. Louis Symphony and Show House Gardens 2002

This wonderful bedroom retreat has the aged look of old plaster walls.
Inviting and unique, this bedroom is rich in character and appeal.

Master Bedroom
Richar Interiors Inc.
Chicago Home and Garden Design House 2003

Photography by David Schilling

The vertical aspect of the room called for the use of a faux boiserie wallcovering to add interest and give the room a more inviting nature. Furnishings and bedding are plush and luxurious in soothing shades of green.

When Color Surrounds
Paula McChesney with Lynne Rutter Murals and Decorative Painting
Coyote Point Museum Auxiliary Decorator Showcase 2003

Due to the room's low ceilings and long rectangular shape, the designers had to balance the architecture and focus the eye's attention to the center of each wall. In order to do this, they devised three levels of silver-leafed mouldings and paneling, hand-painted with chinoiserie flowering trees. All the color in the room is found on the walls, while all the furniture is white, giving the sense of space. Lighting problems were solved by adding up-lights in the room's corners, complimented by the art deco furnishings and custom evening-gown drapes.

Golden Slumber
BJ's Home Accents
Evansville Living Idea Home 2003

The designers set out to make this master bedroom peaceful, dreamy, and romantic, and used the room's faux finish as the foundation for its design. The stunning silk bed ensemble in soft yellow and green tones with a hydrangea motif is slightly feminine, but not overly so. A club chair and ottoman provide the perfect complement to the bedding, and the wall sconces and mounted light fixtures embellish the established theme. An oval pedestal soaking tub is the centerpiece of the master bedroom's elegantly styled bathroom. The walls boast a faux finish that helps the room achieve a classic look. Ornate mirrors and light fixtures add graceful décor.

Applying her philosophy that the architecture of a space should be integrated into and augmented by interior design, this designer used support columns as headboard posters for the floating bed. This third floor bedroom's angles are repeated in the surfaces of the custom cabinetry and the pattern of the custom area rugs. A strong palette serves to reinforce the lines that dominate the room's architectural features.

Butterscotch Stripe
deVlaming Design, Inc.
Charleston Symphony Orchestra League/ASID
Designers' Show House 2003

Photography by E.G. Coyle/Silver Shadows L.L.C.

Photography by E.G. Coyle/Silver Shadows L.L.C.

Photography by E.G. Coyle/Silver Shadows L.L.C.

This designer hung butterscotch-hued wallpaper horizontally to create an exciting design statement. Old heart pine floors exude warmth, a feeling generated throughout the rooms in its sunny tones and casual styling.

Photography by E.G. Coyle/Silver Shadows L.L.C.

Ship Shape
BNK Design Consultants, Inc.
Vassar Show House 2003

A magnificent, hand-painted wallpaper, designed from an archival rendering of a Spanish armada, set the nautical theme for this young girl's bedroom. Soft fabrics, handcrafted Spanish furniture, and period brass tacking work together to create a room both feminine and architecturally defined.

Rosy Outlook
Pauline Vastardis Interiors
Vassar Show House 2003

Roses, fruits, and ivy adorn this tower bedroom, where it's a cool summer evening year round.

Eastern Dreams
Light-Parker Galleries
Vassar Show House 2001

A sophisticated collection of traditional furnishings is set off by a warm and cheerful Oriental print fabric in the bed skirt and window treatment. The collage of patterns and furnishings invites you to relax and dream of wonderful things.

Secret-Garden Fantasy
Images Design and Interiors
Vassar Show House 2000

Mother Nature welcomes children and daydreamers alike to stretch their imaginations as they recline amidst a scene of eternal spring.

Best in Show
Claire Sautter Interior Design, Sarah Kienzle Interiors
Vassar Show House 2002

A young lady's sanctuary reveals her penchant for all things equestrian in the coded language of toile, printed both on the walls and bedspread. The black-and-white theme is punctuated with pink for charming effect.

A Fresh Tradition
Marlboro Interiors
Charlotte Symphony Guild ASID
Show House 2001

This guest bedroom is layered in tradition, yet maintains a sophisticated and fresh look. Soft walls change from blue to green as sunlight moves over the home. Floral curtains, padded headboard, a family portrait, and antique furnishings and accessories complete the look.

Photography by Michael Siede

A Day in the Life of a Princess
Knowlton Associates, LLC
Vassar Show House 2002

©Barry Halkin Photography, Philadelphia

A pretty princess room evokes dreams of castles, kings, carousels and brass rings. Murals of animal princesses were substituted for their human counterparts, creating a whimsical backdrop for this heiress's haven. Miniature furniture was fashioned to fit the occupant.

A Collector's Retreat
Patricia McLean Interiors, Inc.
Atlanta Symphony Orchestra Decorators' Show House 2001

Antique French furniture in warm wood tones anchors a room with an extensive collection of oil canvases that pay tribute to the Great Masters. Couture detailing on upholstery, drapery, and bed fittings contributes to the room's refinement. The writing desk and comfortable places for reading are essential in this bedroom made for a connoisseur of art.

Asian Fusion
Total Design Source, LLC
Shoreline Foundation
Decorators' Show House 2002

©Olson Photographic, LLC

©Olson Photographic, LLC

Oriental and American blend in a style that defines simplicity. Antique Chinese cabinets flank a four-poster bed, surrounded by fabrics that belie an Oriental theme. The combined sitting/sleeping area is as familiar and relaxing as Grandmother's parlor. In the matching master bath, faux finish above the corner whirlpool tub creates the impression of antique tile inset on marble panels.

(Continued on following page)

Rosy Welcome
Knowlton Associates, LLC
Zurbrugg Lourdes Show House 2000

Soft pastels and cheerful florals make this elegant yet cozy master bedroom a welcome retreat.

Master Bedroom and Sitting Area
Vibha Hutchins Design
Suntrust Symphony/ASID Show House 1999

French antiques and continental styling of the bed and window treatments give this master bedroom a European feel with romantic undertones.

His with Hers
Pedro Rodriguez Interiors
Vassar Show House 2000

Pastels add soothing color to a classically furnished master suite.

149

Pretty in Pink
Beekeeper's Cottage in Ashburn
The Loudoun Arts Council's
Designer Show House

A soft, feminine palette sets the stage for sweet dreams, in a guest cottage sure to win repeat visits.

Alan Goldstein Photography / Courtesy of Van Metre Homes

Alise O'Brien Architectural Photography

Iris Bedroom
Diane Breckenridge Interiors, Inc.
Saint Louis Symphony
Show House and Gardens 2003

Lavender and green silk tones make for a romantic and relaxing bedroom. Irises adorn the coverlet and the window sheers, and the plaid pattern is repeated in the bedskirt, canopy, and on the drapes as a band. The final effect is a room full of charm and comfort.

Billy Cunningham Photography

Billy Cunningham Photography

Starting with wonderful architectural advantages – a marble fireplace and wood paneling – the designer built from there. She took blue and white floral fabric and covered the walls and chairs, and created a dust ruffle for the bed. A blue-patterned carpet supports antique furnishings, with a draped four-poster bed for the centerpiece.

Because the Guest is Best
Dean Boslers Furniture Showrooms
Evansville Living Idea Home 2003

Bryan Leazenby/OnSite Images for Evansville Living Magazine

Blue toile was chosen to paper this guest bedroom's walls. The designers used furniture with a reproduction antique look in masculine cherry-toned wood to complement the southern style of the wall covering. The bedding presented a challenge to the designers, who chose a loose floral print to work with, rather than compete with, the busy wallpaper.

Bryan Leazenby/OnSite Images for Evansville Living Magazine

Polka Bow Bath
Carol e. Smith Interior Design
Evansville Living Idea Home 2003

Bryan Leazenby/OnSite Images for Evansville Living Magazine

Bryan Leazenby/OnSite Images for Evansville Living Magazine

The charm of the guest bedroom continues into the guest bath, where the designer wrapped, fringed, and added bow ties to a polka-dot shower curtain. The double-pedestal sink is crowned with matching gold-framed mirrors and the blue and white porcelain plates are used for consistency with the bedroom's styling.

153

"The Philadelphia Story"
Knowlton Associates, LLC
Vassar Show House 2001

©Barry Halkin Photography, Philadelphia

A splendid blend of ivories and muted blues hark back to an era of elegance and social grace. Themed in honor of an area actress, the floral and bird accents are a nod to actress Katherine Hepburn's love of nature.

Photography by Gordon Beall Photography

Azure Slumber
Kelley Interior Design Service, Inc.
National Symphony Orchestra
Decorators' Show House 2001

Photography by Gordon Beall Photography

The designer's intent was to fulfill extravagant taste on a limited budget. Comfort and elegance marry in the azure striated walls and plush bedding. Muslin curtains trimmed with blue velvet and upholstered headboards add interest.

Neoclassic Comfort
Stan Kelly Interiors, Inc.
Traditional Home Showhouse at the Washington
Design Center 2003

In a room devoid of architectural interest, the designer wanted to
draw attention away from the ceiling. In order to do this, he custom-
designed a herringbone-patterned floor and chose a black-and-white
toile print on linen to cover a wall. Clean lines distinguish the
furnishings and a neutral color palette keeps the room fresh.

Photography by Gordon Beall

Photography by Bernardo Grijalva

An Elegant Space for Renewal
Kim Kaneshiro, Allied ASID
ASID California Peninsula Chapter
Designer Showcase House 2003

Photography by Bernardo Grijalva

This romantic bedroom combines
rich woods, soft fabrics, and
interesting shapes to create an old
world style. The feeling in this
room is relaxing and casual, yet
opulent. In the bathroom, an
Italian village mural brings to life
memories of travels in Italy.

Photography by Bernardo Grijalva

Masculine Bedroom
Alan E. Brainerd Interiors, Inc.
Saint Louis Symphony Show House and Gardens 2003

This room emanates a masculine appeal with a faux tortoise wall-covering inset inside the panel molding, crocodile embossed leather club chair and ottoman, and a "turtle table." Warm, dark tones add to this effect, balanced with the fine quality and stylish sensibility of a true gentleman's chamber.

Purely Pleasurable
Charleston Design Center
Charleston Symphony Orchestra League/ASID
Designers' Show House 2001

The light, neutral, monochromatic palette on silk and sheer fabrics gives this inviting guest bedroom an air of elegance and refinement. Subtle dimension is achieved through the used of specific metallic plaster paint techniques on the walls and stenciling on the ceiling.

Beige Impression
Lycknell Interiors
Vassar Show House 2002

A muted palette presents both feminine and masculine appeal in a room that speaks subtly of culture and comfort.

Best for Guests
Stevens Antiques
Vassar Show House 2003

Jaunty angles carry this design, from a corner brass bed angled against a gilded screen, to the unique antique mirror and the asymmetrical window treatments for the lofty room's three outlooks.

Fire Space
Cabbages & Roses LLC
The Loudoun Arts Council's Designer Show House

A three-way fireplace sheds light and a luxurious warmth throughout an expansive stretch of master suite. Along with area rugs, the easy on-off gas unit also acts as a transparent divider between sleeping and sitting areas. A curtain swings down if needed to provide a visual barrier between the two.

Oriental Bed Chamber
Thomas A. Leaver Interior Design
Vassar Show House 2003

An exquisite Chinese bed, circa 1870, became the centerpiece of this room. The bed's 78 individual pieces, hand-carved from catalpa wood, were assembled without screws or nails. To complement it, the room was adorned with a silk embroidery depicting the god of longevity, and the ceiling was papered in an elaborate print.

Sleep Softly
Anne Markstein Interiors
Baltimore Symphony Associates Decorators' Show House 2003

What couple wouldn't want to come home to this bedroom getaway? The white palette and plush textures soothe and promote a good night's rest. The vanity desk, area rugs, bedding, and window treatments were all custom designed and manufactured for this room.

Rosy Retreat
Decorative Interiors & Artistic Surfaces
Shoreline Foundation Decorators' Show House 2002

Draperies imitate a gazebo, while a hand-painted mural provides a garden backdrop for a nap or nightly slumber.
Delicate bursts of pink add blush to the room, and complete the idyllic retreat theme in the form of roses.

©Olson Photographic, LLC

©Olson Photographic, LLC

©Olson Photographic, LLC

160

Dreamy Nursery
Charleston Design Center and Karie Calhoun Interiors
Charleston Symphony Orchestra League/ASID Designers' Show House 2003

A cloud-covered ceiling adds whimsy to this brightly colored nursery. Murals on the attic doors lend a playful atmosphere, while the antiques blended with modern accents create a room that seems to have comforted many generations of children.

Vincent's Room
Interior Dimensions Studio
Vassar Show House 2002

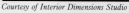

©John Lewis Photography

Courtesy of Interior Dimensions Studio

Courtesy of Interior Dimensions Studio

Courtesy of Interior Dimensions Studio

This room was designed to capture the mood, texture, and symphony of color inspired by van Gogh's painting, "The Bedroom."

Miss Priss
People's Furniture
Evansville Living Idea Home 2003

Valances with a busy burst of pinks, reds, and blues pressed against seafoam green stripes inspired the designer to use a Lexington painted chest with a floral motif. The black iron bed provides a welcome contrast to the floral motif throughout the room.

Beach Boys
West Designs & Interiors
Evansville Living Idea Home 2003

A vacation theme was used to design a little boy's room. The designer stressed the importance of giving an aged look to the room, in order to give it the comfort and history one might find at a family's vacation home. Nautically themed accessories like a functional ship's wheel, message in a bottle, and shells inspire the imagination. Of particular interest is the outdoor fabric hung on the ceiling to resemble a beach umbrella.

Bryan Leazenby/OnSite Images for Evansville Living Magazine

Bryan Leazenby/OnSite Images for Evansville Living Magazine

Safari Fantasy
J. Murray Vise Interior Design
Atlanta Symphony Orchestra Decorators' Show House 2001

The savannah comes to life, both in 3D and impressive hand-painted walls. The furnishings offer a minimal presence, leaving the focus on the awe-inspiring animal assembly. Manufacturer-direct furniture left room in the reasonable budget for an artist's commission and a custom-made bench between the beds.

Old World Nursery
Theresa Russell Interiors, Angela Arcila, and Elisa Perasso
American Lung Association of Florida Designer Showhouse 2003

The designer of this nursery wanted to create a healthy environment for the newborn. Soft shades of green and other natural shades were meant to bring Nature into the room. The hand-painted walls were adorned with old world-inspired frescoes to create an atmosphere of fantasy and gentility. Whimsical accessories from northern Italy and southern France create a fairytale-like environment that would soothe any child.

Tropical Dreams
The Decorators Unlimited Inc.
American Lung Association of Florida Designer Showhouse 2003

The home's magnificent view of the ocean and lush landscape were the inspiration for this room's design. Tropical fabric was used on the draperies and accent pillows to help set up the theme, while warm green and wood tones were chosen to anchor the room. To further capture an island feel, a ceiling detail was designed using bamboo moldings, and the ceiling fan was designed to look like tropical leaves.

Eclectic Grandeur
Donald Lilly Associates Interior Design Inc.
American Lung Association of Florida
Designer Showhouse 2003

The casually elegant styling of this bedroom stays true to the home's architecture. A neutral color palette in combination with eclectic furnishings, artwork, and accessories fill the expansive room. Amethyst and aqua accents add a sense of passion and romance, while a large, hand-carved-glass Venetian chandelier centers the room's grandeur.

©2003 Robert Ludwick/954-785-9919

Restful Terrace
Marcia Cox Interiors
ASID California Peninsula Chapter
Designer Showcase House 2003

©Russell Abraham 2003

©Russell Abraham 2003

The designer used sunny, warm garden colors like yellows, apricots, creams, and greens, linking a small bedroom to the private terrace beyond. Contemporary and traditional pieces were carefully scaled to create a relaxed and harmonious atmosphere. The color scheme from the bedroom is carried onto the terrace, where the designer used casual and comfortable textures. The table base and chairs, scaled for small spaces, are made of a naturally shaded faux rattan and powder-coated iron for year-round outdoor use.

CHAPTER 8
BATHROOMS

Photography by Pat Shanklin

Photography by Pat Shanklin

Le Placard de Eau
Valan & Co.
Charlotte Symphony Guild ASID
Show House 2003

Designers transformed a water closet and adjoining bathroom areas into a luxurious bathroom retreat. Robin's egg blue and champagne tones soothe and add elegance with Documentary print wallpaper and fabulous window treatments, while French antiques enhance the royal air that fills this master bathroom suite. The Chez Perse disguises the commode, adding beautiful form to function.

Photography by Pat Shanklin

Celestial Retreat
Ludi Goodenberger Interior Design
Newport Show House 2000

©Olson Photographic, LLC
©Olson Photographic, LLC

Courtesy of Ludi Goodenberger

Courtesy of Ludi Goodenberger

Silver and gold add sparkle to this serene bathroom, utilizing marbleized layers of white. A leopard print adds whimsy to the vanity's antique piano stool, while jute floor covering grounds the heavenly space. The monochromatic color scheme enhances this narrow but fully functional bathroom, complete with a handy laundry chute.

Classic Sheen
Helen Marshburn, Koehler Kitchen and Bath
Classic American Homes Show House 2000

A cream and neutral-toned color palette gives this luxurious bathroom a fresh feel. Elegance reigns with ballooning drapes and decorative moldings. Light-colored wood cabinets complete the look, adding style and sturdiness.

Sophisticated Update
Gretchen Kaylor Interiors
Charleston Symphony Orchestra League/ASID
Designers' Show House 2002

Courtesy of Wood-Mode/Photography by The Shadowlight Group

While working with the existing cabinetry, fixtures, and tile, this master bath was updated through the use of sophisticated paint finishes, elegant wallpaper, and antique furniture. The asymmetrical swag and jabot window treatment allow for plenty of light, and the organza fabric, detailed rod, and finial enhance the formality of the room. Antique accessories add elegance, incorporating the use of crystal and old monogrammed silver, while the hand-carved Italian chandelier and matching sconces repeat the colors and motif of the rug. Beautiful towels and artwork complete the transformation.

Photography by Leslie Wright Dow

Vanity's Edge
Kelley Interior Design Service
National Symphony Orchestra
Decorators' Show House 2002

Practicality meets a rich sense of style in this master bathroom. For a dramatic effect the designer built a mirrored ledge into the windowsill to create a vanity table.

©2003 Lydia Cutter Photography

Crystal
Cabbages & Roses LLC
The Loudoun Arts Council's
Designer Show House

Alan Goldstein Photography / Courtesy of Van Metre Homes

Drapes demarcate an area set aside for a deep soak. Nearby, a vanity area shares space in custom cabinetry. Crystal fixtures and accessories counterbalance the masculine wood finish.

Fabric Softens
Karie Calhoun Interiors
Charleston Symphony Orchestra League/ASID
Designers' Show House 2000

©Leslie Wright Dow

The designer of this luxurious and romantic bathroom was inspired by the fabric selection in accessorizing the room. Of particular interest is the tub enclosure's accent drapery designed to soften the lines of the room. The French hand-painted chest, window towels, and artwork are all offset by the cool lime faux-finished walls.

Photography by Ed Ritger

Photography by Ed Ritger

Photography by Ed Ritger

Sand, stone, water, light, and wood set a sensual mood
full of movement. The richly textured powder bath takes
its inspiration from the surrounding natural environment of ocean water and brilliant fog to form a space
that boasts glimmering sheen and an earthy sensibility.

Photography by Alexander Vertikoff

A hand-stamped hemp/linen wallcovering highlights the warmth and texture for this elegant bathroom. A custom round mirror that swings to the side for convenience is placed in front of the window to allow for an attractive view upon entering the space while maintaining functionality. Custom mosaic flooring adds character, while the custom oval zebrawood vanity adds an element of the unexpected.

Photography by Alexander Vertikoff

Photography by David Papas—www.papas.com

Using a reproduction tub, handheld shower, and faucets, along with the original sink and toilet, the designers managed to restore this bath to its early 20th century appearance. Walls with layers of translucent blues and greens, Matisse-inspired paintings, and a silk sari curtain add a touch of modernity to the space. The translucent room divider, cabinet doors, and sink shelf were all made of acrylic resin, with leaves and shiny electronic components.

Photography by David Papas—www.papas.com

Serene
Parker West Interiors
Pasadena Showcase 1999

This bathroom exudes an air of tranquility with the use of a subtle palette of gray, green, cream, taupe, and walnut. A custom-designed vanity finishes the style, with its spectacular glass sink and mirror.

A combination of textures and styles gives this master bath a vintage feel. Light green walls help keep the room bright, while the black countertop, bath ledge, and accent tiles add an air of sophistication. The red stool, vase, and candles offset the green walls, giving dimension to the room.

Craftsman's Cubby
Avenue Art & Design
Vassar Show House 2003

Drawing inspiration from the American Craftsman period, wood, simple lines, texture, and natural colors keep the design simple and uncluttered. The walls and ceiling have been finished with a burlap and fresco plaster wall covering. Neutral textiles and art, direct and indirect lighting add to the ambiance of serenity and sophistication.

Blue Bath
Classic Comforts, Inc., Dietrich Construction
Vassar Show House 2003

A mix of old and contemporary details define this space, the tone set by a custom stained-glass window.

Painted Poppies
Pat O'Brien
Baltimore Symphony Associates
Decorators' Show House 2003

Colorful poppies vibrantly decorate this bathroom, featuring a hand-painted mural and shower curtain, a faux white marble countertop, and custom floor tiles. A stylized poppy and wild flower floor cloth, window treatment, artwork, and accessories complete the theme of this room.

©2003 Ian Pitts

©2003 Ian Pitts

European Flair
Alexander Blank Fabrics, Inc.
Baltimore Symphony Associates Decorators' Show House 2001

Photography by John Coyle Jr., Baltimore MD

The contemporary charm of floral chintz, cotton moiré, silk taffeta, and imported lace recreate this spacious bathroom, making one feel pampered and special. Crisp greens, turquoise blue, mango, and marigold sprinkled throughout the room, along with mellow old woods, fill this master bathroom with texture, as well as timeless elegance. The walls of rich "golden" tones set the mood for a romantic, restful bath time. Reality and creativity embrace…character and charm.

Photography by John Coyle Jr., Baltimore MD

Soaking Spot
Lark Interiors, CMD Interiors
Vassar Show House 2001

Crystal balls above, ball feet below, and a handy tray of goodies nearby are perfect antidotes to tired tootsies. Two tones of paint on the walls blend for a sky-like horizon.

Crisp as Linen
Knowlton Associates, LLC
Vassar Show House 2001

Tiled walls and flooring, a mismatched toilet, and 50s collectibles give this bathroom a retro feel. Bright white sheers add a crisp feeling to the room, a topiary adds green, and the shower curtain adds style.

©John Lewis Photography

©John Lewis Photography

Personal Sanctuary
Stephen Dabrowski Interiors & Antiques
Vassar Show House 2001

Starting with an all-white palette presented this designer with a challenge. Introducing fabrics and accessories of color and pattern against a white ground softened the starkness of the porcelain tile. Gold highlights added drama and luxury, while ceiling paper imparted an open-air feeling.

Forward to the Past
Lycknell Interiors
Vassar Show House 2000

A fireplace and a deep tub for soaking form a winning combination in a spacious bath. Wood furnishings and trim add to the inner glow.

©John Lewis Photography

©John Lewis Photography

184

Classic Little Retreat
Classic Design
Tara Drive Decorator Show House 2003

Flowing lines, a touch of romantic highlighting, and earth tones enhance this space. The upholstered walls, shirred ceiling, and rich tones of billowing fabric direct the palette. Elegance and comfort mingle in this cozy niche, where one is uplifted and inspired.

Leaf Me Alone
Linda Wiley Interiors
Vassar Show House 2002

A spacious sitting room, complete with soaking tub and fireplace, completes a luxurious master suite. A theme of foliage recurs throughout, from the mural painting around the fireplace, to the actual plants that enjoy the sunny space.

Richard Smith—HaywardSmith Photography

©John Lewis Photography

A la Chinoise
Lynne Rutter
San Francisco Decorator Showcase 2002

Designed to be a quiet and restful space within a house full of large public rooms, this cozy powder room is private and inti- mate. The custom hand-painted wallcovering is an airy, lighter interpretation of chinoiserie papers popular in the 18th century. Other interesting design elements of the room include the quilted silk window treatment, bamboo chair caning covering the windows, matching faux marble baseboard and antique demi-lune table, and late 18th century hand-carved gilt frame mirror.

Photography by David Papas—www.papas.com

Light in the Morning
Taylor Wells Design
National Symphony Decorators' Show House 1999

Better than a cup of coffee in the morning, this light-filled lady's bath and dressing room wake up the senses and bring life to the day. Beautiful garden views from the windows refresh, while the stylish design energizes. Neutral cream silk faux finished walls create the backdrop for oriental flavored furnishings in black and gold, and a silk "petal" chandelier lends feelings of peace and tranquility.

©2003 Celia Pearson

Photography by Richard Rownak

Grandchildren's Bathroom
Designs by Gerald and Jakeway Finishes
Assistance League of Southern California
Design House 2000

A bathroom carefully styled for the grandchildren features hand-made, glazed porcelain tiles on the walls, floors, and countertops. The window treatment and shower curtain fabric set up the theme around which the custom-finished walls and cabinets revolve. The regulating heat valve in the shower prevents heating and scalding to protect the little ones' delicate skin.

Photography by Richard Rownak

Photography by Richard Rownak

Mediterranean Powder Bath
Designs by Gerald
Assistance League of Southern California Design House 2000

Photography by Richard Rozniak

The designer used tumbled marble and Rossa Verona tile for the walls and floor in a powder room to keep with the home's Italian/Mediterranean style. A hand-painted chest, paper basket, and tissue box add splashes of color to the earthy palette.

CHAPTER 9
BONUS ROOMS
AND SPECIAL SPACES

A Breath of Fresh Air
Rozalynn Woods Interior Design
Pasadena Showcase House 2002

Photography by David Phelps

A poolside cabana was transformed into a light and breezy retreat. The fusion of Caribbean and Asian influences and balance between contrasts makes for a serene and tranquil atmosphere. Transparent curtains give a dreamy and airy quality to the space, while window coverings made of wooden frames attached to ropes preserve that airiness. The custom-designed coffee table is actually a sandbox, perfect for placing drinks. Outside the cabana, the wistful ambiance is maintained through the use of the transparent curtains.

Photography by David Phelps

Photography by David Phelps

Continued on Following page

Photography by David Phelps

Photography by David Phelps

Martha's Retreat
Debra Ferrier Interiors
Vassar Show House 2003

In memory of a dear friend, the designer transformed this third-floor space into a place to escape for peace and solitude. Venetian plastered walls – a faux finish that uses multiple thin layers of plaster, each burnished, with a final finish of metallic gold glaze — create a fresh new colorway juxtaposed by the creamy texture of the carpet, enhancing the mix of metals and sumptuous fabrics.

Exotic Escape
Gregory Oliveri Design & Decorative Arts
Vassar Show House 2003

©John Lewis Photography

An exotic Nepalese god crowns the fireplace, underlined in temple red. A chaise lounge offers a meditative corner for repose and daydreams, beneath several carved Tibetan wood covers. The wainscoting is silk-screened wallpaper from Bradbury & Bradbury.

A Quiet Mind
Dragonfly
Loudon Arts Council's Designer Show House

Photography by Studio Diana

Photography by Studio Dian

Any room can be easily transformed into a personal sanctuary. Here, the original den was redesigned into a meditation room. The mind is quiet, the body still, and the spirit strong. Amidst tranquil colors, luxurious fabrics, and Chinese antiques, one finds sanctuary, peace, and an abundance of style. Because the room was located in the lower level of the home, the designers created the illusion of a window by incorporating a large Chinese screen and window treatments of striped silk shantung and burlap on a bamboo pole.

Created as a feminine retreat, this room creates the impression that one has just entered a conservatory. Framed botanical prints fill in where windowpanes are wanting, and a super-sized mirror doubles what natural light is emitted.

Ornithologist Field Tent
Your Space, Inc.
San Francisco Decorator
Showcase 2001

The designer imagined an ornithologist as the occupant of this interior/exterior space. Even inside a tent, space seems almost endless, with crisp lines and a window covered only by a sheer curtain. The birds painted on the tent walls, some hanging feathers, and a cushion that looks like a bird's nest reveal this occupant's preferred flight of fancy.

davidduncanlivingston.com

davidduncanlivingston.com   *davidduncanlivingston.com*

Day Dreamin'
Sonja Willman Designs
St. Louis Symphony
Show House & Gardens 1999

Faux climbing vines suit the cozy styling of a dreamer's retreat, where the world slips away, and comfort takes over, lending itself to fanciful reflection.

John Martinelli Photography

A morning room connected to the master bedroom brings occupants awake with vibrant colors designed to set the tone for the day. Touches of black add punch to the red and yellow theme, and a breakfast table provides another function for the space.

Neutral tones and richly textured fabrics give this room a relaxing, luxurious feel. What woman wouldn't love to curl up on the canopied daybed with a good book, candles lit?

A window seat and an "altar" to Nature set the scene for heavenly reflection.

Queen of Everything
Genevieve Roberts Home Collection
Vassar Show House 2002

Enter the area of the forties, when young girls were groomed to be feminine, cultured, and prepared for their future.

Stranded ... I Wish
Interior Dimensions
Vassar Show House 2002

Artist David Bruce Michener created the ultimate castaway getaway in this room, where one can fantasize about being alone, or share the fantasy with the perfect other.

Day Dream
Thomas A. Leaver Interiors
Vassar Show House 2000

A collection of favorite things blend for an aura of escape in this lofty day room.

Private Collection
Kitty McFarland Interiors
Vassar Show House 2000

Choosing art as an alternative investment has led to the creation of a special room, high up on the third floor. Here the homeowners enjoy their art-lover's wish come true.

Going Up!
Interior Dimensions
Vassar Show House 2000

Imagine you're at the top of the world, in the Empire State Building's observatory. Here the static electricity is so strong lovers might find their lips spark when they kiss.

Potting Room
Sonja Willman Designs
ASID Cardinal Glennon Guild Designers' Show House 2002

The designer of this room wanted to give the impression of a space that had evolved over time. The potting room is a bit off-center but cozy and user-friendly, expressing the owner's passion for the art of gardening and all that it encompasses.

Photography by Quadra Focus

In this wine cellar, a faux bois treatment was used on the original plaster beams to give them the look of heavy timber. Custom slipcovers on the formal chairs cover up a clashing material and give a more casual feel to the room. Centuries-old limestone pavers create an authentic, aged atmosphere, while a custom-designed "candelier" adds warmth and depth to the design. Good friends, good wine, and good food – you may never want to leave this wine cellar.

Spiffy Spot
Smith & Childs Custom Framing,
Rebecca F. Brinks Designs
Vassar Show House 2002

This laundry room was created
to be enjoyed, not dreaded.

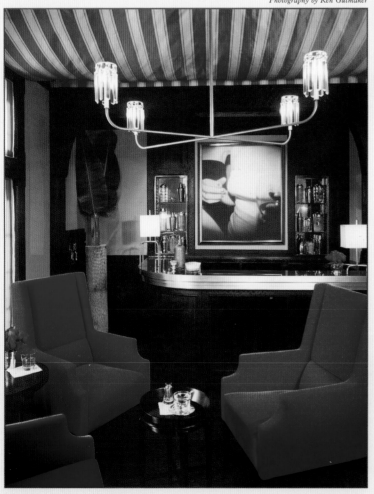

Bar None
Your Space, Inc.
San Francisco Decorator Showcase 1999

A sexy residential bar was paneled in black painted glass with
butterscotch paint. To make reflective walls that were not
mirrored, the woodwork was all stained a dark espresso brown.
The ceiling was tented with the same watermelon-striped silk
taffeta that was used to make the custom roman shades and
matching mohair was used for the club chairs.

Disappearing Act
Intertect Design Consultants, Inc.
Charleston Symphony Orchestra League ASID
Designers' Show House 2001

www.trippsmithphotography.com

State of the art equipment and sophisticated styling combine to create an eclectic, imaginative, and intimate media room. Plasma technology made it possible for the designer to hide a television behind a custom-made two-way mirror, seen only when turned on. Existing architectural elements like the heart-pine flooring and beaded-board walls provided a warm atmosphere, while shimmery fabrics helped to add sophistication.

Welcome to the New Millennium
Parker West Interiors
Pasadena Showcase 2000

This media room provides a dramatic entrance into the 21st century with a liquid crystal panel that allows for central control of the lighting, audio, and visual systems. Casual furniture groupings allow for pure relaxation. The room's original dressing closet provides a functional bar and snack area, and like the bathroom, features the combination of ceramic tile, glass, and limestone. Fiber optics are featured in the star ceiling, art sculpture, and bathroom vanity countertop.

Photography by Alexander Vertikoff

Photography by Alexander Vertikoff

Photography by Alexander Vertikoff

Photography by Alexander Vertikoff

Photography by Alexander Vertikoff

Photography by Alexander Vertikoff

Remember blanket tents? Tree houses? Those spaces filled a need for intimacy, for privacy. This petite screening room is the grown-up reinterpretation of the secretive getaway. Conceived as a gentleman's retreat, it is tucked away in a corner of the third floor, far from the hustle and bustle of family life.

Mass Media
Nancy Werneken Interior Design
Tara Drive Decorator Show House 2003

Richard Smith—HaywardSmith Photography

Richard Smith—HaywardSmith Photography
Richard Smith—HaywardSmith Photography

Richard Smith—HaywardSmith Photography

This media room is best described as warm and inviting, a place where the family entertains and gathers. Shades of golden ochre, moss, and deep raspberry with classic black were chosen to enhance the stunning natural maple custom cabinetry, which elegantly houses state of the art media equipment. The system's speakers are hidden behind fabric panels within the ceiling. A collection of Barry Miller photographs, featuring musicians, candid portraits of children, and architectural perspectives creates a fun and personal atmosphere that enhances the elegance and comfort of the home.

Pied-À-Terre
Anthony Wilder Design/Build, Inc.
Fall Design House, by *Traditional Home* 2002

Innovation, comfort, and tranquility combine to create an urban retreat carefully designed to support a contemporary lifestyle. The space is kept open and pure, all the while accommodating multiple demands with a multimedia center, kitchen, library, and dining area. Balanced and harmonious, this pied-à-terre is a welcome escape from the hassles of everyday living.

Loft 3: A Study in Wabi Sabi
Rink Reynolds Diamond Fisher Wilson, P.A.
Suntrust Symphony/ASID Show House 2003

Photography by Joseph Lapeyra

Photography by Joseph Lapeyra

The designers of this loft developed a concept using the principles of Wabi-Sabi, which stems from Zen philosophy. These principles revolve around finding beauty in the simple, serene, and subtle elegance of objects made with natural materials, especially those that display the effects of aging. Designers used a monochromatic palette to enhance the feeling of serenity with deep, warm tones. The natural combines with the high-tech for an unforgettable balance.

Photography by Joseph Lapeyra

Children's Atelier
Home Works Design & Supply
Vassar Show House 2003

Magical and fanciful, hand-painted murals and decorative finishes give the walls and ceiling dimension and texture in this treetop playroom. A custom floor cloth lends color and a wipe-able surface for spills. Coordinated fabrics soften the windows and upholstery. The rest – teddy bear parties and sleepovers – are supplied by imagination.

©John Lewis Photography

©2003 Robert Ludwick 954-785-9919

Caribbean Elegance
Robb & Stucky
American Lung Association of Florida
Designer Showhouse 2003

This sitting room's design was inspired by the tropical ambiance of the Caribbean and the European settlers who incorporated their 18th century furnishings with the island way of life. The designer chose bright colors, architectural elements in handcrafted white painted wood, woven carpets, and colorful prints to complete the look.

©2003 Robert Ludwick 954-785-9919

Her Sitting Room
Jeffrey Sachs Designs Inc.
American Lung Association of Florida
Designer Showhouse 2003

A woman needs a place for herself, a place where she can reflect and be surrounded by her mementos collected during travels throughout her life. A 150-year-old chest, hand-painted in shades of plum, teal, and butter, is the center-piece of the room. The hand-painted border adds a Mediterranean flavor to the space.

Tuscan Cellar
Designs by Gerald
Assistance League of Southern California Design House 2002

A Tuscan-inspired landscape embraces this cellar, comfortably styled to create a space for gatherings of friends and family. Rich, warm colors promote conversation and ease, while old world accessories give a sense of history.

Photography by Richard Rownak

DECORATOR
RESOURCE GUIDE/CONTRIBUTORS

ASID Pasadena Home Tour
Carol Cobabe
ASID Pasadena Chapter
1000 E Walnut, Suite 108
Pasadena, CA 91106
626-795-6898

Alexander Blank Fabrics, Inc.
Marietta B. Ries and Judi Bradshaw
Timonium, MD
410-561-2331

Alan E. Brainerd Interiors, Inc.
Alan E. Brainerd
St. Louis, MO
314-726-1984

Amy B. Severin Design
Havertown, PA
610-662-0876

Anne Markstein Interiors
Anne Markstein
Millers, MD
410-343-1330

Anthony Wilder Design/Build, Inc.
Anthony Wilder; Kary Ewalt, ASID;
and KT Wilder
Cabin John, MD
301-907-0100/301-907-4536
www.anthonywilder.com

Architextures Interior Design, LLC
Saint Louis, MO
314-961-9500
www.architexturesllc.com

Artistic Design
Angela Arcila
FL
954-593-5178

Artistic Surfaces
Betsy Demarco
Hamden, CT
203-230-2165

Ateliart
Elisa Perasso
Ft. Lauderdale, FL
954-349-3043

Avant Architects
Lori Krejci and Austin Riley
Omaha, NE
402-493-9611

Avenue Art & Design
Barbara Wasserman
East Tawas, MI
989-362-0277
www.avenueartanddesign.com

Ayres Bartholomew Interiors
James Taylor, Industry Partner ASID
Palm Beach, FL
561-832-1021/561-573-2079
jtaylor@abifurn.com

B² Group
Judy Buchanan
Branford, CT
203-481-5472

BJ's Home Accents
Bill Fortson and John Clements
Newburgh, IN
812-853-7381

BNK Design Consultants, Inc.
Karen Spewak, Barbara Bottinelli, Joy
Kendall
West Conshohocken, PA
610-941-2943

Barrie Vanderpoel Designs
New York, NY
212-472-0405

Beekeeper's Cottage in Ashburn
Nancy Hilliard and Anne Carrington
Ashburn, VA
703-726-9411
www.beekeeperscottage.com

Bergeson Design Studio, LLC
Robin Bergeson
Ashburn, VA
703-723-7557

Bernadette V. Upton Interior Design
Bernadette V. Upton, ASID
Lake Park, FL
561-845-5433/561-313-6413
ecodecor@hotmail.com

Bloomingdale's Design Studio
Moira McHugh, Susan Shaub, ASID
King of Prussia, PA
610-337-6249

Bordet Interiors
Marc Bordet
Quincy, MA
617-773-7786

Brian Foster
Philadelphia, PA
215-790-0144

Bruce Norman Long Interior Design
Princeton, NJ
609-921-1401
New York, NY
212-980-9311

CMD Interiors
Christine Duval, IFDA
Berwyn, PA
610-647-8045

Cabbages & Roses LLC
Michelle Becraft
Ashburn, VA
703-858-7373

Carol A. Jackson Interiors, Inc.
Carol Jackson-Stanford, Allied ASID
843-884-0620
www.carolajacksoninteriors.com
carol@carolajacksoninteriors.com

Carol e. Smith Interior Design
Carol Smith Gerth
Newburgh, IN
812-853-9585

Carolyn Platt Antiques
Berwyn, PA
610-644-0100

Charleston Design Center
Joyce Cerato, Allied Member ASID
Charleston, SC
843-722-4550
www.charlestondesigncenter.com

**Cinda Vote Design Group/
Office Design Center**
Cinda Vote
Evansville, IN
812-473-2020

Claire Sautter Interior Design
Claire Sutter, Allied Member ASID
Huntingdon Valley, PA
215-938-8535
www.cskinteriors.com

Classic Comforts, Inc.
Marge Farbman, ASID
Newtown Square, PA
610-356-7766

Classic Design
Sandra Murphy, IDS
Duxbury, MA
781-829-4922
www.classicdesignnet.com

Cox Interior Design
Wayne D. Cox
Gulph Mills, PA
610-834-0401

Creative Design Solutions, Inc.
Heather Littlewood Wojick, ASID
Charlotte, NC
704-849-0488

Cynthia Cericola-Hartz Interiors
Cynthia Cericola-Hartz, Allied Member
ASID
Haverford, PA
610-649-5499

DGI Design Group
Diane Gordy, CID, ASID, IIDA
Bethesda, MD
301-229-9500
www.dgidesigngroup.com
dgordy@dgidesigngroup.com

Dakota Wall Arts
Michelle Saad, ASID Industry Partner
Palm Beach, FL
561-254-5114
DakotaWallArts@msn.com

Dean Bosler's Furniture Showrooms
Dean and Karen Bosler
Evansville, IN
812-476-8787

Debra Ferrier Interiors
Debra Ferrier
Centreville, DE
302-427-9106

Decorative Interiors
Laurie Dragonoff
Hamden, CT
203-230-0934
www.greatstylenow.com

The Decorators Unlimited Inc.
Bob Martin and Rosa DiCarlo, ASID
Palm Beach Gardens, FL
561-625-3000
www.decoratorsunlimited.com
info@decoratorsunlimited.com

Design 2 Interiors
Eleanore Berman, ASID and Sharon
Daroca, Allied ASID
San Jose, CA
408-270-4497
www.design2interiors.com

Design Details, LLC
Regina Garcia, Allied ASID, CKD
Charleston, SC
843-406-8705

Design Galleria Kitchen & Bath Studio
Atlanta, GA
404-261-0111
www.designgalleria.net

Design Solutions, Inc.
Joni Zimmerman, CKD, CBD; Pam
Kanewske; Linda Watson
Annapolis, MD 21401
800-894-7349
410-757-6100
Easton, MD 21601
410-820-6770
www.dsikitchens.com

Design Works Creative Partnership, Ltd.
Steven M. Hefner, ASID
Delray Beach, FL
561-272-6855

Designers Furniture & Interiors
Susan Rubin, Nancy O'Hara, Eileen
Linton
Norristown, PA
610-279-8980

Designs By Gerald
Gerald Sowell
Los Angeles, CA
323-461-2271
www.designsbygerald.com

Devine Designs, Inc.
Eileen Devine, Cynthia Fisher
Wayne, PA
610-688-6518
www.devinedesignsinc.com

deVlaming Design, Inc.
Caroline deVlaming, Allied Member
ASID
Charleston, SC
843-853-0601/853-270-5200

Diane Breckenridge Interiors, Inc.
Diane Breckenridge
Clayton, MO
314-727-2323

Diane Hughes Interiors
Diane Hughes, Allied Member ASID
Rye, NH
603-964-9543

Dietrich Construction
Newtown Square, PA
610-353-4726

**Donald Lilly Associates
Interior Design Inc.**
Donald Lilly, ASID
Jupiter, FL
561-746-5010/561-452-5777
Dlilly2468@aol.com

Dragonfly
Kimberly Hessler
Reston, VA
703-467-8675
www.dragonflyantiques.bz

Elisa Perasso
Ft. Lauderdale, FL
954-349-3043

**Elisabeth A. Lane, ASID,
Interior Design**
Villanova, PA

Ethan Allen Evansville
Ruth Roat, Jennifer Scales,
and Laura Tower
Evansville, IN
812-479-0821
www.ethanallen.com

Ethan Allen Interiors
Melissa Mejasic, Kate Savino, Barbara
Brolly, Kim Wilkins, Michele Larkins, Lisa
Cooley, Liz Weidner, and Jessica Deal
Paoli, PA
610-644-2200
www.ethanallen.com

Evaline Karges Interiors
Tay Ruthenberg and Kip Farmer
Evansville, IN
812-477-4790

Exquisite Designs and Décor
Patricia Shelton
Leesburg, VA
703-443-9200
www.exqsitdesign.com

Faith Ashley Interiors
Hanover, MA
671-306-0038
faith_ashley_1999@yahoo.com

Flair Design Group
Charlotte Healy
Emerald Hills, CA
650-366-8584

The French Lemon
ML Wilcox, Gina Foley
Wayne, PA
610-687-6744

Gary Roeberg Designer
Cherry Hill, NJ
856-751-1840

Genevieve Roberts Home Collection
Voorhees, NJ
856-566-7500

**Goldthorpe & Edwards,
Interior Design & Decoration**
J. Wesley Goldthorpe and Anne L.
Edwards
Haddonfield, NJ
856-979-7422/215-868-0191

**Gregory Oliveri Design
& Decorative Arts**
Gregory Oliveri, Christopher Hansen
Philadelphia, PA
215-243-9411

Gretchen Kaylor Interiors
Gretchen Kaylor, Allied Member ASID
Mt. Pleasant, SC
843-884-0436
gkaylor149@comcast.net

Group 3
Michael G. Ruegamer, Nancy Wilkinson
Exton, PA
610-321-2401
www.group3arch.com

**Group3 Architecture.
Interiors. Planning.**
Mike Ruegamer, Eloise Smith, Christina Scharf
Hilton Head, SC
843-689-9060
www.Group3arch.com

Hilary Musser Interior Design
Bryn Mawr, PA
610-525-8041

Home & Garden Culture
Kennett Square, PA
610-388-6300
www.homeandgardenculture.com

Home Works Design & Supply
Jane Norley
West Chester, PA
610-430-7337
www.homeworkshome.com

Images Design and Interiors
Lydia Diaz-Kirchner
Doylestown, PA
215-489-1597

Inside Outlook Custom Interiors
Joanna Lyon, IFDA
Exton, PA
610-363-2737
www.insideoutlook.com

Interior Dimensions Studio
David Bruce Michener
Boca Raton, FL
561-241-2894
www.davidbrucemichener.com

Interior Expressions
Laura Ronis
Leesburg, VA
703-669-1587

Interior Landscapes
Stanley H. Willauer, Jr.,
Lawrence Benjamin
Philadelphia, PA
215-991-9039

Intertect Design Consultants, Inc.
Beth Huntley, ASID
843-557-0777
Bhuntidc@aol.com

J & L Interiors
Julie Hoffmann and Lori Marsan
Aldie, VA
703-327-9050

J. Murray Vise Interior Design
J. Murray Vise, IIDA
Atlanta, GA
404-892-9708

Jakeway Finishes
626-253-1255
www.jakewayfinishes.com

Jan Kyle Design
Westwood, KS
913-677-3290
http://jankyledesign.tripod.com

Jeffrey Dean, Ltd.
Jeffrey Dean Soulges
Philadelphia, PA
215-248-5555
www.jeffreydeanltd.com

Jeffrey Sachs Designs Inc.
North Palm Beach, FL
561-622-2163

John Cole Interior Design
Los Angeles, CA
310-659-9034

Joseph Hittinger Designs
Joseph Hittinger, ASID, CID, IIDA,
Associate AIA
Palo Alto, CA
650-322-8388

Justine Sancho Interior Design
Justine Sancho
Bethesda, MD
301-718-8041

Karen Brown Interiors
Tampa, FL
813-340-2085

Karen L. Byrne, Interior Designs
Berwyn, PA
610-647-3853

Karen Padgett Prewitt
Charleston, SC
843-722-8125

Karie Calhoun Interiors
Karie B. Calhoun, Allied ASID
Charleston, SC
843-207-1638

Kelley Interior Design Service, Inc.
Kelley Proxmire
Bethesda, MD
301-320-2109

**Kim Kaneshiro Interior
and Garden Design**
Kim Kaneshiro, Allied ASID
Los Altos, CA
650-948-7135
www.kaneshirodesign.com
kaneshirodesign@att.net

Kitty McFarland Interiors
Aston, PA
610-358-5446

Knowlton Associates, LLC
Lesa C. Knowlton, IFDA, Allied Member ASID
Haddon Heights, NJ
856-547-8282
www.knowltonassoc-interiordesign.com

Lark Interiors
Judi Larkin, IFDA
Paoli, PA
610-889-9981
www.larkinteriors.com

Lea Matthews Furniture & Interiors
Joan Fraser
Evansville, IN
812-474-4266

Light-Parker Galleries
Conshohocken, PA
610-828-1875
www.lightparker.com

Linda Wiley Interiors
Malvern, PA
610-640-9691

Lisa Davenport's Home Gallery
Lisa Davenport, Allied Member ASID
Glastonbury, CT
860-659-8476
www.lisadavenport.com

Lisa Newman Interiors
Lisa Newman Paratore
Barrington, RI
401-246-2026
www.lisanewmaninteriors.com

Ludi Goodenberger Interior Design
Newport, RI
401-849-3270

Lycknell Interiors
Gloria Steward Lycknell, Designer
Wyomissing, PA
610-372-3363
www.lycknellinteriors.com

**Lynne Rutter Murals
and Decorative Painting**
Lynne Rutter
San Francisco, CA
415-282-8820
www.lynnerutter.com

Maisel Interiors
Denise Maisel
Palo Alto, CA
650-493-5352

Marcia Cox Interiors
Marcia Cox, ASID
Menlo Park, CA
650-322-4307

Margery Wedderburn Interiors
Margery Wedderburn
Vienna, VA
703-757-5001
www.margerywedderburninteriors.com

Marlboro Interiors
Betty F. Kohn, Allied Member ASID
Charlotte, NC
704-365-1393

**Marshall Field's Interior
Design Studio**
Brian Clay Collins, FASID; Ray
Dymond; and Rovanna Corte
Southfield, MI
248-443-6244
www.marshallfields.com

Maurice E. Weintraub Architect
Wayne, PA
610-688-1336
www.mewarchitect.com

McChesney Design Studio
Paula McChesney
San Mateo, CA
650-343-9610

Melanie Ward, Inc.
Madison, CT
203-421-5586

Micheline Laberge, ASID
Sarasota, FL
941-924-1778
www.michelineasid.com

Miho Kahn Interiors
West Chester, PA
610-793-3274

Miller Stein
Marcia Miller, ASID; Steven Stein,
ASID;
Janice Marcus, Allied Member ASID
Los Altos, CA
650-559-1705
www.millerstein.com

Morris Black Designs Studios
Dan Lenner, CKD, CBD, and Pat
Donohue, CKD
Bryn Mawr, PA
610-525-1025
www.morrisblack.com

NMP, Inc.
William Boal
West Chester, PA
215-552-8835

Nancy Werneken Interior Design
Nancy Werneken
Medfield, MA
508-359-1598

Nesting Feathers Design Guild
Claire Daniels, Francine Dunigan
Malvern, PA
610-408-9377
www.nestingfeathers.com

Nu-Way
South Norwalk, CT
203-866-2555

**Office Furniture USA
Division of Fuller Office Furniture**
David Bloom
East Hartford, CT
800-367-3634
www.fulleroffice.com

P & H Interiors Inc.
Mariel Rubin, ASID with Julie Harris
Coral Springs, FL
954-341-7335
www.pnhinteriors.com
mariel@pnhinteriors.com

Paoli Fabric
Berwyn, PA
www.paolifabric.com

Parker West Interiors
Greg Parker
South Pasadena, CA
626-403-5008
www.parkerwestinteriors.com

Pat O'Brien
Cockeysville, MD
410-628-7107
themuralist@comcast.net

Patricia McLean Interiors, Inc.
Atlanta, Georgia
404-266-9772
www.mcleaninteriors.com

Patricia Spratt for the Home
Old Lyme, CT
860-434-9291

Pauline Vastardis Interiors
Pauline Vastardis, FIFDA, IIDA Associate, Cathy Ruff, IFDA
Moorestown, NJ
856-866-1625
www.pvinteriors.com

Pedro Rodriguez Interiors
Pedro Rodriguez, FASID
Bala Cynwyd, PA
610-660-9611

Penelope Rozis
San Francisco, CA
415-387-8844
www.pennyrozis.com

People's Furniture
Stan Flittner and Mary Riley
Evansville, IN
812-476-7661

Personal Style, LLC
Melissa Kradas
Madison, CT
203-245-8018

Pickens Homes LLC
Susan Pickens
Evansville, IN
812-461-0123

Plum Interior Design
Eileen Marcuvitz
Lincoln, MA
781-259-1740

Rebecca F. Brinks Designs
Rebecca Brinks
Havertown, PA
610-446-0689

Richar Interiors Inc.
Richar
Chicago, IL
312-951-0924
www.richarinteriors.com

**Rink Reynolds Diamond
Fisher Wilson, P.A.**
Larry Wilson, ASID, AAID; Kim
Sutton, ASID, IIDA;
Rebecca Davisson, ASID, IIDA
Jacksonville, FL
904-396-6353
www.rrdfw.com

Robb & Stucky
Sarah Frisco, ASID
Boca Raton, FL
561-347-1717
sarahfrisco@robbstucky.net

Rozalynn Woods Interior Design
Rozalynn Woods and Michaela Scherrer
Pasadena, CA
626-441-1022
rozalynnwdesign@aol.com

The Rutt Studio on the Main Line
Julie Ann Stoner, ASID, CKD
Wayne, PA
610-293-1320
www.ruttstudioonthemainline.com

SJ Designs
Sherry Joyce
Redwood City, CA
650-365-3433
www.sjdesigns.com

Sarah Kienzle Interiors
Sarah Kienzle
Morrestown, NJ
856-231-1331
www.cskinteriors.com

Schneider/Fox Associates
Luba Fox Alexander, ASID, CID
John J. Schneider, ASID, CID
Carmel, CA
831-624-7978

The Secret Garden
Barbara Ulrich and Kelly Hutchins
Newburgh, IN
812-858-9128

Shelley Gordon Interior Design, Ltd.
San Francisco, CA
415-674-9543

Silver Moon Studio
Lisa M. Wehler
Media, PA
610-891-7770

Smith & Childs Custom Framing
Donique Browsh, Sharon Kates
Ardmore, PA
610-896-8330

Sonja Willman Designs
Manchester, MO
636-256-0011

Sorella's Decorating, LLC
Madison, CT
203-245-5118

Stacey Lapuk Interior Design, Inc.
Stacey Lapuk, ASID, CID
San Rafael, CA
415-499-1228
www.staceylapukinteriors.com

Stan Kelly Interiors, Inc.
Stan Kelly
Washington, D.C.
202-234-6922

**Stephen Dabrowski
Interiors & Antiques**
Newtown Square, PA
610-353-4109

Stevens Antiques
Carol Lehman
Frazer, PA
610-644-8282
www.stevensantiques.com

Style House
Karin Taylor
Haverford, PA
610-254-0902

Susan Dearborn Interiors, Inc.
Wellesley Hills, MA
781-235-2920
www.dearborndesign.com

Susan Fredman & Associates, Ltd.
Lani Myron
Northbrook, IL
847-509-4121
www.susanfredman.com

Susan Harter, Muralist
Arlington, MA
617-501-1320
www.susanharter.com

t.k. i.d.
Tracey M. Kessler
San Francisco, CA
415-447-2749
www.tk-id.com

Taylor Wells Design
Taylor Wells
Riverdale, MD
800-895-2768/301-864-9457
twellsdesign@aol.com

Teal Michel, ASID
Charlotte, NC
704-554-7035

Theresa Russell Interiors
Theresa Bartolo, Allied Member ASID
Boca Raton, FL
561-852-0620
trdesignbuild@aol.com

Thomas A. Leaver Interiors
Media, PA
610-565-3385

Toby Strogatz Interiors at Xcessories
Philadelphia, PA
215-483-9665
www.xcessoriesinc.com

Total Design Source
Chantal Lawrence
Essex, CT
860-767-8965

Tracey Robb Interiors
Ardmore, PA
610-896-0992

Tucker Publishing Group
Kristen K. Tucker
Evansville, IN
812-426-2115
www.evansvilleliving.com

Valan & Co. Interior Design
Elizabeth K. Grigg, Allied ASID, CKD, CAPS
Lindy Kovalanchik
Charlotte, NC
704-372-0090

Valentine Interiors Design & Decorating Shop
Helene Valentine
Clinton, CT
860-669-7625

Vibha Hutchins Design
Vibha Hutchins, ASID
Jacksonville, FL
904-739-6655
www.vibhahutchins.com

West Designs & Interiors
Liddy West
Newburgh, IN
812-858-9998

Wheeler Design Group
Marian Wheeler and Matthew Leverone
San Francisco, CA
415-863-7766
www.wheelerdg.com

Willem Racké Studio, Inc.
San Francisco, CA
415-252-1341
www.willemrackestudio.com

Wood-Mode
Kreamer, PA
877-635-7500
www.wood-mode.com

Your Space, Inc.
Charles De Lisle, Marion Philpotts, and Jonathan Staub
San Francisco, CA
415-565-6767
www.your-space.com

SHOW HOUSES

ASID California Peninsula Chapter Showcase House

Proceeds from the Showcase were donated to Peninsula Volunteers and the educational and community service efforts of ASID-California Peninsula Chapter.

Chapter Office
Menlo Park, CA
650.323.6791
www.asidcap.org

ASID Cardinal Glennon Guild Designers' Show House

The Cardinal Glennon Guild and the American Society of Interior Designers presented the Show House to benefit The Department of General Surgery SSM Cardinal Glennon Children's Hospital.

Cardinal Glennon Children's Hospital
Saint Louis, MO
314.577.5605/800.269.0552
www.glennon.org

Alliance Children's Theatre Guild Christmas House

In its 29th year, this event contributes to the success of the Alliance Children's Theatre. The organization entertains families, encourages creativity, and introduces children to the joy of live theatre through performances, workshops, and volunteer opportunities for all ages.

Alliance Theatre Company
Atlanta, GA
404-733-4650
www.alliancetheatre.org

American Lung Association of Florida Designer Showhouse

The mission of the American Lung Association of Florida is to promote lung health and prevent lung disease. Proceeds from the association's first Designer Showhouse went toward funding local education programs and research to find a cure for asthma and other lung diseases.

American Lung Association of Florida
West Palm Beach, FL
800-330-5864
www.inhaleexhale.org

American Red Cross Designer Show House

The American Red Cross Designer's Show House has been a bi-annual event since 1986. The area's top interior designers contribute time and talent to showcase their work and raise funds for the American Red Cross.

Palm Beach Central Headquarters
West Palm Beach, FL
561-833-7711
chapterhq@redcross-pbc.org

Anne Arundel Medical Center Auxiliary Designer Show House

The auxiliary was established in 1944 as a volunteer group to serve the hospital. Volunteers are an integral part of AAMC's mission of providing patient-centered, high quality health care services to the community and in raising funds for many hospital projects.

Anne Arundale Medical Center
Annapolis, MD
443-481-5050
www.aa-healthsystem.org

Assistance League of Southern California Design House

This annual design house benefit raises funds for their league services, which help over 110,000 individuals of all ages each year.

Assistance League
Hollywood, CA
323-469-1973
www.designhousela.org

Atlanta Symphony Orchestra Decorators' Show House

For thirty-three years, the Atlanta Symphony Associates have organized show houses to benefit the Atlanta Symphony Orchestra. They have contributed over eight million dollars in the last eight years.

Show House
404-733-4935
dsh@woodruffcenter.org
www.decoratorsshowhouse.com

Baltimore Symphony Associates Decorators' Show House

This volunteer arm of the Baltimore Symphony Orchestra comprises over 250 associates who provide time, talent, and energy to benefit the Education Programs of the BSO. The associates' have been serving the BSO since 1942 when they began as the Women's Committee.

Baltimore Symphony Associates
Baltimore, MD
410-783-8023
www.baltimoresymphony.org

Beaufort Academy Designer Show House

The event benefits a fully accredited college preparatory school that is incorporated not-for-profit and dedicated to providing an excellent learning environment for the motivated student.

Beaufort Academy
Beaufort, SC
843-524-3393
www.beaufortacademy.org

Brevard Symphony Orchestra's Designer Show House

PO Box 361965
Melbourne, FL
321-242-2024
www.brevardsymphony.com

Center for Family Development Designers' Showcase

This non-profit organization is under the direction of the Legionaries of Christ. Since 1993 it has offered an intensive marriage preparation program, marriage enrichment workshops, mother-daughter and father-son activities, parenting series, and a leadership program for young boys and girls.

Our Lady of Bethesda Retreat Center
Center for Family Development
Bethesda, MD
301-365-0612
www.bethesdacfd.org

Charleston Symphony Orchestra League/ASID Designers' Show House

The league works with the CSO Board to provide music education programs, support audience development, and through fundraising projects. The CSOL also procures and refurbishes used musical instruments and lends them to talented students who otherwise would not have the opportunity to participate in school musical activities.

Charleston Symphony Orchestra
Charleston, SC
843-723-7528
www.charlestonsymphony.com

Charlotte Symphony Guild ASID Show House

The guild creates, develops, and promotes an interest in symphonic music and provides financial and volunteer support to the Charlotte Symphony Orchestra Society, the Charlotte youth symphonies, and symphonic educational activities.

Charlotte Symphony Orchestra
Charlotte, NC
704-972-2003
www.symphonyguildcharlotte.org

Chicago Home & Garden Design House

The design house was created by the magazine's editorial team, Orren Pickell Designers & Builders, and Chicago-based interior designer Richar to benefit the Junior League of Chicago. The Junior League's community-centered work focuses on empowering at-risk families, through mentoring, advocacy, and education.

Junior League of Chicago
Chicago, IL
312-664-4462
www.jlchicago.org

Coyote Point Museum Auxiliary Decorator Show House

This museum works to inspire a lifelong commitment to act responsibly in caring for the earth. The museum provides engaging, educational experiences for a diverse, multi-generational Bay Area community through wildlife, gardens, exhibitions, and programs that relate to the global environment.

Coyote Point Museum
San Mateo, CA
650-342-7755

Deborah Hospital Foundation Show House

This event was created in 1995, coordinated by the Foundation's New Jersey Region, with help from the Medford, Moorestown, Riverfront Chapters, and many volunteers. Funds support the Deborah Heart and Lung Center in Browns Mills, NJ, a 161-bed teaching hospital specializing in the diagnosis and treatment of heart, lung and vascular diseases.

Deborah Hospital Foundation
Browns Mills, NJ
609-893- 3372
www.deborahfoundation.org

DOG HAUS – SPCA Decorators' Show House

The first DogHaus in 2003 benefited the Pennsylvania SPCA for support of education and animal rescue efforts.

Pennsylvania SPCA
Philadelphia, PA
215-426-6300
www.spcadoghaus.com

Evansville Living Idea Home

The first event in 2003 was made possible by the coordinated efforts of the *Evansville Living Magazine*, Pickens Homes, and Vectren to showcase the products and services of Evansville-area businesses and to benefit the Junior League of Evansville. Ticket proceeds also benefited Little Lambs in its mission to assist at-risk mothers make healthy choices for their families.

Tucker Publishing Group
Kristen K. Tucker
100 NW Second St., Suite 220
Evansville, IN 47708
812-426-2115
www.evansvilleliving.com

Florida Orchestra Guild, St. Petersburg Designer's Showcase

The St. Petersburg Orchestra Guild was organized in 1963 to serve the St. Petersburg area, providing volunteer services and financial support to the orchestra through the development of attendance, cultural awareness, and interest.

The Florida Orchestra
Tampa, FL
813-286-1170
admin@floridaorchestra.org

House Beautiful Celebrity Showhouse

This event benefits The Children's Action Network, which uses the power of the entertainment community to increase awareness about children's issues and to make them a top priority in everyday life through extensive public education campaigns, community-based programs, and policy initiatives.

Children's Action Network
Los Angeles, CA
310-470-9599
www.childrensactionnetwork.org

Hudson River Designer Showhouse

The 2000 Hudson River Designer Showhouse benefited Women's Services of the Union State Cancer Center at Nyack Hospital, which houses a unique and innovative Appearance Center & Mastectomy Boutique with breast prostheses, wigs, and other resources for patients undergoing cancer treatment.

Nyack Hospital
Nyack, NY
845-348-8500
www.nyackhospital.org

The JCC Designer Show House

Organized by the Jewish Community Center of the North Shore, dedicated to maintaining and enriching Jewish identity; enhancing personal, social and physical development, developing leadership ability, and participating in and contributing to the welfare of the total community.

Jewish Community Center of the North Shore
Marblehead, MA
781-631-8330
www.jccns.org

Junior League of Detroit Designers' Show House

This women's organization is committed to promoting voluntarism, developing the potential of women, improving communities through the effective action, and elevating the lives of children. They initiate and participate in community-based collaborative partnerships that broaden the educational, cultural, recreational, and health opportunities for area children.

The Junior League of Detroit, Inc.
Grosse Pointe Farms, MI
313-881-0040
www.jldetroit.org

Junior League of Nashville, Decorators' Show House

This women's organization promotes voluntarism and reaches out to women of all races, religionsm and national origins who demonstrate an interest in and a commitment to voluntarism.

The Junior League of Nashville
Nashville, TN
615-269-9393
www.jlnashville.org

Kansas City Symphony Designer Show House

Founded in 1961, the Junior Women's Symphony Alliance (JWSA) coordinates this annual event.

Kansas City Symphony
Kansas City, MO
816-471-1100
www.kcsymphony.org
www.showhouse.org

Kips Bay Boys & Girls Club Decorator Show House

For over 85 years, Kips Bay has helped to shape the lives of thousands of young children throughout the New York metropolitan area. The organization serves over 8,700 members at seven locations, two of which are located in homeless shelters, offering an array of services, educational programs, and opportunities to children ages 6 to 18. In 2003, Kips Bay organized its 31st annual Decorator Show House.

Kips Bay Office of Marketing & Special Events
New York, NY
212-213-2800
www.kipsbay.org

Lake Forest Showcase House & Gardens

Proceeds from the 2003 event benefited the Infant Welfare Society of Chicago, which is dedicated to providing health services for disadvantaged women and children.

Infant Welfare Society of Chicago
Chicago, IL
312-751-2800
www.infantwelfare.org

The Loudoun Arts Council's Designer Show House

Three organizations pulled together to sponsor the first show house in 2003, hosted by the council in partnership with Lansdowne on the Potomac, Van Metre Homes, and élan Magazine

The Loudon Arts Council
Leesburg, VA
703-777-7838
www.loudounarts.org

Lourdes Show House

This show house benefits patient care services and community outreach programs at Our Lady of Lourdes Medical Center in Camden and Lourdes Medical Center of Burlington County in Willingboro, NJ.

Lourdes Health Systems
Camden, NJ
856-482-4965
www.lourdesnet.org

Marin Designers Showcase

Presented by the Auxiliary of Marin Nexus, which addresses the needs of over 1,000 non-profit organizations in Marin, CA.

Auxilary of Marin Nexus
San Rafael, CA
415-479-5710
www.marinnexus.org

Middlesex County YMCA, Lyman Homestead Showhouse

The showhouse is organized by the women's board committee of the YMCA. All proceeds from the showhouse benefit the Northern Middlesex County YMCA in its mission to serve the community.

Northern Middlesex County YMCA
Middletown, CT
860-347-6907

National Symphony Orchestra Decorators' Show House

The Women's Committee was founded in 1941 to provide financial and service support to the Orchestra's education, outreach, and artistic programs. The NSO Decorators' Show House is the principal fundraiser of the Women's Committee and has raised over $9 million for the NSO since its inception in 1973.

John F. Kennedy Center for the Performing Arts
Washington, DC
202-416-8000

Newport Show House

Since 1994 the Newport Showhouse Guild has produced three spectacular showhouses raising funds for Newport County charities

Newport Show House Guild
Newport, RI
www.Newportshowhouse.org

Old York Historical Society Decorator Show House

The Old York Historical Society is dedicated to the promotion and preservation of the history of the York region for the education and enjoyment of the public.

Old York Historical Society
York, Maine
207-363-4974/207-363-4021
www.oldyork.org

Omaha Symphony ASID Designer Show House

This event is a joint effort by The Omaha Symphony Guild and the Nebraska-Iowa Chapter of the American Society of Interior Designers. Funds go to education programs and scholarships for area design students.

Omaha Symphony
Omaha, NE
402-342-3836
www.omahasymphony.org
www.omahasymphonyshowhouse.org

Pasadena Showcase House

The Pasadena Showcase House for the Arts (PSHA) is a non-profit California corporation. The annual benefit combines the efforts of PSHA members and designers, and has resulted in cumulative donations in excess of $12 million to the Los Angeles Philharmonic, schools, and other local non-profit organizations.

PSHA
San Marino, CA
626-578-8500
www.pasadenashowcase.org

Princeton Junior League Show House

The Junior League of Greater Princeton is a non-profit women's organization committed to promoting voluntarism, developing the potential of women, and to improving the community through the effective action and leadership of trained volunteers. Its purpose is exclusively educational and charitable.

Junior League of Greater Princeton
Trenton, NJ
609-771-0525
www.jlgp.org

St. Louis Symphony Show House & Gardens

All proceeds from this event directly benefit the Saint Louis Symphony Orchestra and its music education and outreach programs.

St. Louis Symphony Orchestra
St. Louis, MO
314-533-2500/800-232-1880
www.saintlouissymphony.org
www.symphonyshowhouse.com

San Francisco Decorator Showcase

This event is the major fundraiser for financial aid at San Francisco University High School, an school recognized as one of the top fifty high schools in America. Since its inception twenty-seven years ago, the event has raised over $7 million for the UHS financial aid budget, providing tuition assistance to more than 20% of the students annually.

San Francisco University High School
San Francisco, CA
415-447-3117
www.decoratorshowcase.org

Sarasota ASID Designer Showhouse

Profits help provide funds to The Boys & Girls Clubs of Manatee and Sarasota Counties and scholarships at Ringling School of Art and Design and the University of South Florida in Sarasota.

ASID Florida North Chapter
Sarasota, FL
941-954-4454
www.resources.com/ASID/asidfln

Shoreline Foundation Decorators' Show House

The foundation creates opportunities for recreational and life enrichment in the Connecticut shoreline region through innovative programs and events, building a community that nurtures friendships and values the physical, emotional, and social well being of residents of all ages.

Shoreline Foundation, Inc.
Guilford, CT
203-458-6612
www.shoreline.org

Suntrust Symphony/ASID Show House

This show house benefits The Guild of the Jacksonville Symphony Association, which contributes financial support to the nationally renowned Jacksonville Symphony Orchestra and music education projects for school children.

Jacksonville Symphony
Jacksonville, FL
904-358-1479
www.jaxsymphony.org

Tara Drive Decorator Show House

The Tara Drive Show House benefited The Susan G. Komen Foundation, which raises money for breast cancer research, education, screening, and treatment. It is credited as the nation's leading catalyst in the fight against breast cancer.

Susan G. Komen Foundation
Dallas, TX
972-855-1600/972-855-1605
http://showhousemedia.com/

Universal Design Demonstration Home

The Center for Universal Design with the collaboration of AARP organized this event to provide universal design, training, and consulting services to the Casino Reinvestment Development Authority of Atlantic City, New Jersey. This was one of three initiatives with the overall goals to provide universally designed homes and neighborhoods in Atlantic City and to allow individuals with disabilities to remain in their homes.

The Center for Universal Design
North Carolina State University
Raleigh, NC
800-647-6777/919-515-3082
www.design.ncsu.edu/cud/

Vassar Show House

Operated annually by the Philadelphia Vassar Club since 1967, the Vassar Show House is the oldest East Coast decorator show house event. Each year, proceeds from the benefit provide financial assistance for area students attending Vassar College, with more than $3 million dollars raised and distributed to well over 800 students.

Philadelphia Vassar Club
Bryn Mawr, PA 19010
610-527-9717
www.vassarshowhouse.org

WBNA Povidence Design House

The West Broadway Neighborhood Association organizes neighbors and businesses on the West Side of Providence to preserve and promote their diverse, historic, urban community as a safe, vibrant, and sustainable place to live, work, and play.

West Broadway Neighborhood Association
Providence, RI
401-831-9344
www.wbna.org

Washington Design Center

Each spring and fall, The Washington Design Center unveils a new Design House, an on-site designer show house. Every new season offers a new theme with beautifully appointed rooms created by prominent local interior designers. Proceeds from Design House special events have benefited many local and national organizations.

Washington Design Center
Washington, DC
202-646-6118
www.merchandisemart.com/dcdesigncenter/